Advertising & Marketing Checklists

Advertising & Marketing Checklists

77 PROVEN CHECKLISTS TO SAVE TIME & BOOST ADVERTISING EFFECTIVENESS

Ron Kaatz

NTC Business Books
a division of *NTC Publishing Group* • Lincolnwood, Illinois USA

1990 Printing

Published by NTC Business Books, a division of NTC Publishing Group.
©1989 by NTC Publishing Group, 4255 West Touhy Avenue,
Lincolnwood (Chicago), Illinois 60646-1975 U.S.A.
Manufactured in the United States of America.
Library of Congress Catalog Card No. 88-62121

9 0 VP 9 8 7 6 5 4 3 2

With love to Ian Lester and Michelle Rose...
the newest additions to top all of my checklists and charts.

Table of Contents

Contents

Contents

Foreword

If you picked up this book expecting to find lots of prose to wade through before you got to the good stuff, think again.

Ron Kaatz wastes neither his words nor your time...because the basic premise of *Advertising & Marketing Checklists* is to help you make faster, better and more profitable advertising and communications' decisions the moment you open the cover.

How often has a title been all sizzle while the book was of little substance.

Not here.

What Ron promises, he delivers.

Whether you are trying to develop a commercial that sells, decide in which medium to place your money, determine whether to use public relations, develop a direct marketing or sales promotion program, hire a research company, or negotiate to win, there is something here for you. As a matter of fact, after 20 minutes of scanning the galleys, I discovered "The Advertising Executive's Income Tax Saver"; it reminded me of a deduction I should have been taking for the past three years!

Since 1984, when I took early retirement as chairman of Marsteller, Inc. (Marsteller Advertising and Burson-Marsteller Public Relations, a division of Young & Rubicam, Inc.), and arrived on the Northwestern campus, the ad industry has realized true "future shock." With the multitude of mergers and acquisitions, it is totally impossible to keep track of the players without a scorecard. More than a third of the homes in the country now have *both* cable television and a VCR...and zip and zap to their heart's content. A major marketer who once was satisfied with a simple national advertising plan now tailors 200 separate local programs. And John Wanamaker's famous remarks about not knowing which half of his store's advertising was working has been revised to read, "Now, I don't even know *if* half of my advertising is working!"

In this environment, whether you are faced with the simplest or the most complex problem, you need all the help you can get. Fortunately, Ron is at the right place at the right time with a very important and well-written book. Actually, the word *book* leaves much to be desired. It is really a "survival kit." And Ron is the perfect person to help you survive. In 30 years at Leo Burnett Co., CBS and J. Walter Thompson, Ron was always admired by his associates because they knew a call to him would produce a fast and effective solution to a problem. He is a superb presenter, and, fortunately, Northwestern's Medill School of Journalism was able to grab him to teach advertising.

Whether you pay for it by cash, check or credit card, *Advertising & Marketing Checklists* will be the best investment you've made in a long time—an investment that will pay you deep dividends.

Richard C. Christian, *Associate Dean*
J. L. Kellogg Graduate School of Management, Northwestern University,
and Past Chairman, Marsteller, Inc.

Introduction

The idea for *Advertising & Marketing Checklists* was born 30 years before I sat down to write it.

In June 1957, I graduated from Northwestern University's Medill School of Journalism (to which I have now returned to teach) and went to work in the media department at Leo Burnett.

From my earliest days at Burnett, I was constantly asked for "things." All kinds of "things": names, numbers, lists, charts, maps, reasons why, strengths of, weaknesses of, opportunities for, alternatives to, etc., etc., etc.

I soon discovered that whenever I was asked a question, I would be asked the same question by someone else a few weeks later.

It was this that led to the birth of "The Bible"—13 thick black notebooks that contained everything about anything. What distinguished them from everyone else's thick black notebooks was that only I knew what was in them. The tabs simply said Bible—Book I, Bible—Book II, Bible—Book III, and so forth. I think I labeled it that way because I wasn't sure what would end up in each of the books. I also knew that if my friends at Burnett really understood what was in them, they would begin to be permanently borrowed from my office.

The Bible was a living source which I constantly supplemented and updated. When asked a question, I could retrieve all relevant information from The Bible...update it...add any new thoughts...and have an answer in a fraction of the time required by starting from scratch and reinventing the wheel.

I soon discovered that the information everyone found most helpful came in the form of checklists and charts. They were the easiest to use, and you could interact with them in presentations.

The Bible followed me from Leo Burnett to the CBS Television Network and then on to J. Walter Thompson. File folders gradually replaced the big black books and I began to identify what was inside them, but the basic idea of constantly updated, easily accessed and easy-to-use checklists and charts remained.

As the maze of material we in advertising must constantly wade through has multiplied, the need for checklists and charts has grown. A frustrated advertiser summed up the need best when he said, "I asked what I should consider when thinking about sponsoring an event and was given a 45-page report and three magazine articles to read! I don't have time for that. Can't someone simply give me a list of all the pros and cons...what to look for and what to look out for?"

That's what *Advertising & Marketing Checklists* is all about.

It is an information center in a book. It is partly a cookbook of tasty problem-solving recipes and partly a road-map to make your trips on the job easier.

Today, the advertising industry is being transformed by mergers, acquisitions and growing profit pressure. There is a new focus on sales promotion and direct marketing. As the population changes, top-down marketing is giving way to bottom-up regional planning. Advertisers must also deal with increasing costs, new creative approaches, rate negotiating, single source data, peoplemeters, audience fragmentation, new media options, zapping and zipping...and the basic question, "Is my advertising doing anything?"

In a nutshell, everyone in advertising must make more critical decisions about more issues affecting more dollars and more people than ever before. And all in less time!

Introduction

Advertising & Marketing Checklists focuses on these issues. Its simple-to-follow structure will let you work smarter and make your work easier. Its many tools will help you assess your advertising needs, get new ideas, and create advertising. . .maneuver through the media. . .handle public relations, direct marketing, sales promotion, and research. . .prepare effective presentations. . .and write and negotiate successfully. It will help you get new business and establish and maintain better client relations. It will assist you in getting a job. It will take some of the travail out of travel, and help you keep more of what you make by saving on your income tax. You'll even find a section of frequently requested forms that never seem to be around when you need them.

Advertising & Marketing Checklists is for everyone involved in advertising. It is for the multinational corporation with a $500 million annual advertising budget and for the suburban merchant who spends $5,000 in his home community newspaper.

But it is not meant to be read and put away on the shelf. It is an interactive problem solver that is to be taken apart, copied, filled in, and added to. Where there are questions to be answered, answer them. Where there are spaces to be filled in with your ideas and thoughts, fill them in. Probe your thinking and try to understand your responses. You may want to take parts of this book into meetings with you, or carry parts in your pocket or attache. Do it! Use this book in any way that helps you work smarter and more efficiently.

I have had fun writing *Advertising & Marketing Checklists* and I hope you have fun using it. I said it was interactive, and if you would like to write me with your thoughts, questions or suggestions for future checklists and charts, please do so.

Enjoy!

Part I

The Basics: Why Do We Advertise? How Do We Get Ideas?

Whether you are General Motors Corporation or a Chevrolet dealership in Sioux Falls, South Dakota...Procter & Gamble Co. or Sunset Foods in Highland Park, Illinois ...John Hancock Life Insurance Co. or The McRae Insurance Agency in Winston-Salem, North Carolina, you have asked yourself these questions more than once. These 8 checklists and charts all focus on the basics: how you might benefit from advertising, how you can assess your advertising needs, and how you can come up with fresh, new ideas to accomplish these needs and make your business grow.

1. 33 Reasons to Advertise
2. The 13-Point Advertising and Public Relations Needs Assessor
3. The Ben Franklin Advertising Option Evaluator
4. The Advertising Effectiveness Idea Provoker
5. Coming Up with a New Idea: Part I
6. Coming Up with a New Idea: Part II
7. 11 Reminders for Developing New Ideas in a Group
8. Marketing a New Product? A 15-Point Early Warning System

33 Reasons to Advertise

One of the most frequently asked questions by everyone who is concerned about the cost of doing business is "Why should I advertise?" In the first column, check off all those reasons why you believe *your competition* advertises. In the second column, check off every reason why *your business* might benefit from advertising. Your responses will not only help provide you with a rationale for advertising, but they will also point to new directions that your advertising perhaps should take.

	Why Does Competition Advertise?	Why Should We Advertise?
1. To attract new customers	☐	☐
2. To increase the frequency of use	☐	☐
3. To increase the number of different uses	☐	☐
4. To increase the number of different users	☐	☐
5. To increase the quantity purchased	☐	☐
6. To increase the frequency of replacement	☐	☐
7. To increase the length of the buying season	☐	☐
8. To switch customers from other companies or brands	☐	☐
9. To bring a family of brands together	☐	☐
10. To turn a disadvantage into an advantage	☐	☐
11. To attract a new generation of users	☐	☐
12. To create, enhance or maintain image, prestige or leadership	☐	☐
13. To introduce something new	☐	☐
14. To reintroduce something old	☐	☐

33 Reasons to Advertise

	Why Does Competition Advertise?	Why Should We Advertise?
15. To introduce or announce a new company	☐	☐
16. To support a promotion	☐	☐
17. To promote an entire industry	☐	☐
18. To open doors for the sales force	☐	☐
19. To introduce a new company name	☐	☐
20. To reposition a company	☐	☐
21. To rise above the competition	☐	☐
22. To gain professional approval or endorsement	☐	☐
23. To maintain professional approval or endorsement	☐	☐
24. To improve employee morale	☐	☐
25. To boost sales force productivity	☐	☐
26. To develop sales leads	☐	☐
27. To conduct research	☐	☐
28. To enter new markets	☐	☐
29. To offer brochures and reports	☐	☐
30. To support a cause	☐	☐
31. To oppose a cause	☐	☐
32. To combat unfavorable publicity	☐	☐
33. To announce something fast	☐	☐

The 13-Point Advertising and Public Relations Needs Assessor

Every business must continually reassess its performance. This includes an appraisal of the degree to which its advertising and public relations accomplish its agreed-upon objectives. *The 13-Point Advertising and Public Relations Needs Assessor* helps you conduct your appraisal.

1. What are the goals of your business?

   _____

   _____

2. To what degree have these goals been met?

   _____

   _____

3. Overall, what are your business's greatest strengths?

   _____

   _____

4. What have been your major problem areas?

   _____

   _____

5. If you had to do it all over again, what would you do differently?

   _____

   _____

6. Where do most of your present customers come from?

   _____

   _____

7. What customers that you do not now serve would you like to have?

_____

_____

8. What form has your past advertising and public relations taken?

_____

_____

9. How much have you allocated to spend on advertising and public relations in the past?

_____

_____

10. What are your priorities over the next 12 months in terms of the growth of your business?

_____

_____

11. What objectives do you want your advertising and public relations to accomplish?

_____

_____

12. How much will it cost you to accomplish these objectives?

_____

_____

13. How will you know if your advertising and public relations succeeds in meeting these objectives?

_____

_____

The Ben Franklin
Advertising Option Evaluator

Ben Franklin developed a very simple technique to evaluate the pros and cons of any set of circumstances.

First, he divided a sheet of paper in half.

Second, he listed all the factors supporting a given position on the pro side and all of the factors opposing it on the con side.

Third, he "weighed" each pro against each con. Whichever side outweighed the other determined his course of action.

The Ben Franklin Advertising Option Evaluator lets you apply this same technique in deciding whether or not to invest in a given advertising opportunity or try a new advertising approach.

ADVERTISING OPTION

Pros	Cons
1. _____	1. _____
2. _____	2. _____
3. _____	3. _____
4. _____	4. _____
5. _____	5. _____
6. _____	6. _____
7. _____	7. _____
8. _____	8. _____
9. _____	9. _____
10. _____	10. _____

4 The Advertising Effectiveness Idea Provoker

Before you ever begin to solve a problem or come up with a new idea, you must first define your problem. You must look at what you are doing now and determine how well it is accomplishing what you have set out for it to do. *The Advertising Effectiveness Idea Provoker* is a first step in this process. It is aimed at uncovering any concerns you might have about your advertising program. These concerns can then act as the springboard in helping you develop a new idea.

Read the following statements and fill in the blank space at the end.

☐ I am basically satisfied with my advertising program.

☐ It appears to showcase my product (or service) well.

☐ It seems to be conveying to my customers what I want to tell them.

☐ It seems to be efficient.

☐ I believe it is doing an effective job.

☐ I only wish that _____

_____

_____

_____

_____

5 Coming Up with a New Idea: Part I

Advertising has been defined as a business of constantly developing new ideas to communicate to the consumer. With appreciation to James Webb Young, here is a technique which has proven helpful to many who struggle daily to come up with that big new creative, media, research or promotion idea.

First. . . . . . Gather together absolutely everything that can possibly help you. Search your own mind, dig through all of your files, and seek whatever might be available from other outside sources.

Second . . . Examine all of this information and think about how each piece relates to every other piece *and* to your problem. Massage the material well and look at it from every angle.

Third. . . . . "Out of sight, out of mind." Forget about your problem and go do something else. While your conscious mind is engaged in some other activity, your subconscious will have a chance to work for you in peace and quiet. Don't rush the process. . .be patient and relax.

Fourth . . . . "That's it!". . .you will suddenly shout as the new concept comes to you often in the most unexpected place at the least expected time.

Fifth . . . . . Now the work of refining your idea begins. When the joy of discovery has died down, begin to work with your newly conceived concept. Build upon it, refine it, try it out, until it becomes that new workable, winning idea.

6

Coming Up with a New Idea: Part II

Sometimes you try and try and still just can't come up with that new idea. Your mind needs a few gentle nudges. When you find yourself in this predicament, try a few idea starters like these.

1. Can you break a rule and do the unexpected?

   How?_____

   _____

2. Can you make someone say "Why didn't I think of that?"

   How?_____

   _____

3. Can you combine two small ideas into one big one?

   How?_____

   _____

4. Can you associate the unknown with the known?

   How?_____

   _____

5. Can you associate the untried with the accepted?

   How?_____

   _____

6. Can you associate the traditional with the new?

   How?_____

   _____

7. Can you demonstrate something?

   How?_____

   _____

8. Can you appeal to the sense of sight?

   How?_____

   _____

9. Can you appeal to the sense of sound?

   How?_____

   _____

10. Can you appeal to the sense of smell?

    How?_____

    _____

11. Can you modify *when* something is normally done?

    How?_____

    _____

12. Can you modify *how* something is normally done?

    How?_____

    _____

13. Anything else?

    How?_____

    _____

7

11 Reminders for Developing New Ideas in a Group

Have you ever wrestled with a problem all by yourself, only to have someone say "Why don't we . . . ?" Chances are you had your answer. The best ideas often come about when minds meet in an idea-generating session. But a productive session must encourage, not hinder, the thought process. These 11 reminders will help you reach the best ideas every time.

1. Make certain that your meeting place is comfortable and informal.

2. When you are trying to nourish the mind, you must not neglect the body. Have plenty of beverages and snacks around.

3. Select a good leader who will act as your "tour director."

4. Clearly define the problem when the meeting begins.

5. Set an agenda and time schedule and stick to it.

6. Keep detailed notes of all the ideas that are expressed.

7. Permit no criticism of any ideas or negative reactions to suggestions.

8. Let one idea build on and expand into another.

9. Keep all the participants actively involved in making contributions.

10. Encourage an off-the-wall, free-wheeling discussion. Remember that you are concerned with the quantity, not the quality, of ideas you come up with.

11. Once the meeting is over, apply your normal business judgment in sifting through all of the ideas, targeting the best prospects and developing them.

Marketing a New Product?
A 15-Point Early Warning System

Each year, companies introduce thousands of new products or services. Unfortunately, only a small percentage of them will succeed. Often, no real consumer need or desire exists for them. In other cases, a market may exist, but a business cannot be developed. This *15-Point Early Warning System* will help you evaluate whether or not to consider developing a new product or service.

	YES	NO
1. Is there a need or a consumer desire for the product?	☐	☐
2. Is it practical?	☐	☐
3. Is it unique?	☐	☐
4. Is the price right?	☐	☐
5. Is it a good value for the money?	☐	☐
6. Can your company make money on the product?	☐	☐
7. Does it appeal to a wide enough market?	☐	☐
8. Or, is there a smaller market segment that is anxious to have it?	☐	☐
9. Does it have a long potential life, or is it just a fad?	☐	☐
10. If it is a fad, can it make a short term profit?	☐	☐
11. How great is the threat of competition?	☐	☐
12. Is there a ready, reputable and reliable facility to manufacture, package and get it to market?	☐	☐
13. Does it have a market that can be effectively and efficiently reached by advertising, sales promotion and/or public relations?	☐	☐
14. Is it legal?	☐	☐
15. Is the payoff worth the time and money involved?	☐	☐

Part II

Creating the Advertising

Effective advertising wins sales and an increased share of your customers' pocketbooks. If it also wins creative awards, so much the better—but a shelf of awards should not be your primary goal. Advertising that sells begins with a carefully spelled-out road map called the Creative Strategy Statement. It considers the customers you want to reach...the benefits your product or service will deliver to them...and the impact you want your advertising to have on them. The 11 checklists and charts in Part II will guide you in developing the Creative Strategy Statement and then executing a selling print ad or broadcast commercial.

The Creative Strategy Statement Planning Worksheet

Before you write word one of your advertising copy, you must review all of the research and analyze all of the facts on your product or service and its market, customers and competition. From this background, you will put together a single-page creative strategy statement. It clearly and concisely identifies the purpose of your advertising, whom you want to reach, what you want to convey to your audience and how you want your message to be received. *The Creative Strategy Statement Planning Worksheet* provides you with a format and instructions for preparing this important document.

Purpose: A brief statement of what you want the advertising to accomplish or what you want the consumer to do after exposure to the message.

_____

_____

_____

_____

Target Consumer: A series of short descriptive phrases that define to whom you want to talk in demographic, psychographic, lifestyle and/or product usage terms.

_____

_____

_____

_____

Key Benefits: A clear and simple statement of those real or perceived consumer needs and wants which the product or service will satisfy or that consumer problem which the product or service will solve better than will its competition.

_____

_____

_____

_____

The Creative Strategy Statement Worksheet

Reason Why:

Those significant and unique qualities which convince the target consumer that the product or service can and will deliver the promised benefits.

_____

_____

_____

_____

Tone:

The feeling, style or approach of the advertising that will create a living personality for the product or service.

_____

_____

_____

_____

The Consumer "Take Away":

The total reaction you want from the consumer—in the consumer's own words—after seeing or hearing the message. Did you get through?

_____

_____

_____

_____

31 Ways in Which Advertising Appeals to the Consumer

To successfully communicate with the consumer, advertising must appeal to the individual's needs, wants, desires, hopes and ambitions. In developing advertising strategies, use this checklist to note appeals used by you and your competition, and then check off appeals you might consider using in the future.

	Appeals Used by Competitors	Appeals We Use	Appeals We Might Use
1. Taste or hunger	☐	☐	☐
2. Comfort	☐	☐	☐
3. Beauty	☐	☐	☐
4. Attractiveness to others	☐	☐	☐
5. Well-being of loved ones	☐	☐	☐
6. Adventure or bravery	☐	☐	☐
7. Social status	☐	☐	☐
8. Approval of others	☐	☐	☐
9. Superiority over others	☐	☐	☐
10. Physical well-being	☐	☐	☐
11. Security	☐	☐	☐
12. Fear	☐	☐	☐
13. Fun and games	☐	☐	☐
14. Economy	☐	☐	☐

Advertising Appeals to the Consumer

	Appeals Used by Competitors	Appeals We Use	Appeals We Might Use
15. Efficiency	☐	☐	☐
16. Cleanliness	☐	☐	☐
17. Safety	☐	☐	☐
18. Happiness	☐	☐	☐
19. Romance and/or sex	☐	☐	☐
20. Excitement	☐	☐	☐
21. Rest	☐	☐	☐
22. Ambition	☐	☐	☐
23. Sympathy	☐	☐	☐
24. Guilt	☐	☐	☐
25. Avoidance of pain	☐	☐	☐
26. Entertainment	☐	☐	☐
27. Curiosity	☐	☐	☐
28. Rest	☐	☐	☐
29. Dependability	☐	☐	☐
30. Durability	☐	☐	☐
31. Peace	☐	☐	☐

35 Ways in Which Advertising Gets Attention & Communicates

Advertising uses many different techniques and combinations of techniques to attract attention and communicate with the consumer. This checklist focuses on the variety of devices available to both you and your competitors, and helps you to consider new options for future campaigns.

	Techniques Used by Competitors	Techniques We Use	Techniques We Might Use
1. Humor	☐	☐	☐
2. Real-life dramatizations	☐	☐	☐
3. Slices of life	☐	☐	☐
4. Testimonials	☐	☐	☐
5. Guarantees	☐	☐	☐
6. Comparisons	☐	☐	☐
7. Problem solving	☐	☐	☐
8. Characters	☐	☐	☐
9. Talking heads	☐	☐	☐
10. Recommendations	☐	☐	☐
11. Reasons why	☐	☐	☐
12. Facts	☐	☐	☐
13. News	☐	☐	☐
14. Emotion	☐	☐	☐
15. Cartoons	☐	☐	☐
16. Animation	☐	☐	☐
17. Charts	☐	☐	☐

	Techniques Used by Competitors	Techniques We Use	Techniques We Might Use
18. Computer graphics	☐	☐	☐
19. Claymation	☐	☐	☐
20. Music	☐	☐	☐
21. Symbols	☐	☐	☐
22. Animals	☐	☐	☐
23. Contests and sweepstakes	☐	☐	☐
24. Offers	☐	☐	☐
25. Exaggeration	☐	☐	☐
26. Glamour	☐	☐	☐
27. Personalities	☐	☐	☐
28. Spokespersons	☐	☐	☐
29. 800 numbers	☐	☐	☐
30. The product alone	☐	☐	☐
31. The product in use	☐	☐	☐
32. Different uses for the product	☐	☐	☐
33. Effects of *not* using the product	☐	☐	☐
34. Before and after	☐	☐	☐
35. The package as the star	☐	☐	☐

12

A Road Map for Moving from an Idea to an Ad That Sells

Once you are convinced you have that great advertising idea, your work is just beginning. You must translate the idea into an advertisement or commercial that sells. *A Road Map for Moving from an Idea to an Ad That Sells* is a "moving checklist." Refer to it frequently, as you would to a road map. Next to each point, check whether you are keeping on the right road. Then, in the space beneath each point, indicate where you seem to be taking a detour and what you need to do to get back on track.

	YES	NO

1. Have you learned everything you could possibly learn about your product or service? ☐ ☐

_____

_____

2. Have you learned everything you could possibly learn about your customer—the person who will use, buy or influence the purchase of your product or service? ☐ ☐

_____

_____

3. Have you written to your customer as you would write to a real-life person, and not just a research statistic? ☐ ☐

_____

_____

4. Have you promised to deliver a real benefit to your customer and then backed this up with real reasons why he or she will receive this benefit? ☐ ☐

_____

_____

5. Have you recognized that your customer's time is valuable and gotten right to the point? ☐ ☐

_____

_____

Moving from an Idea to an Ad

	YES	NO

6. Have you made certain that what you said relates specifically to you and not to your competition? ☐ ☐

_____

_____

7. Have you avoided saying more than was necessary? ☐ ☐

_____

_____

8. Have you written with excitement and enthusiasm so your customer will say... "They really believe in what they're selling"? ☐ ☐

_____

_____

9. Have you rewarded your customer by making it easy and fun for him to spend time with your advertising? ☐ ☐

_____

_____

10. Have you never forgotten for a moment that the product or service is the star of your advertising, not the advertising itself? ☐ ☐

_____

_____

9 Tips for Creating More Effective Print Ads

An effective magazine or newspaper ad wins awards from the consumer's pocketbook—not just from art competitions. While there is no simple formula for creating advertising that automatically sells, the following tips are fundamental to the success of any ad. If you cannot answer "Yes" to every one of these questions, the odds say you will have considerable trouble communicating your message from the magazine or newspaper page to the consumer's active mind. To prevent this, take a moment to think about how you can change each "no" to a "yes."

	YES	NO
1. Is the message clear at a glance? Can you quickly tell what the ad is all about?	☐	☐
2. Is there a benefit in the headline?	☐	☐
3. Does the illustration support the headline?	☐	☐
4. Does the first line of copy support or explain the copy or illustration?	☐	☐
5. Is the ad easy to read and easy to follow?	☐	☐

Creating More Effective Print Ads

	YES	NO
6. Is the type large and legible?	☐	☐

_____

_____

| 7. Is the advertiser clearly identified? | ☐ | ☐ |

_____

_____

| 8. Have all excess words, phrases or even ideas been deleted? | ☐ | ☐ |

_____

_____

| 9. If there is a coupon or clip-out, is it easy to remove or easy to get? | ☐ | ☐ |

_____

_____

Source: *Strategic Advertising Campaigns,* by Don E. Schultz, Dennis Martin and William P. Brown (1984)

How to Avoid the Most Common Mistakes in Writing Copy

In their book *Which Ad Pulled Best?* Philip Ward Burton and Scott C. Purvis isolated six factors that tended to separate copy which generated strong consumer response from copy that was less effective. Use this 6-point checklist to monitor your own advertising. Note those areas where you feel your copy is falling short and comment on how it might be improved.

	YES	NO

1. Does the copy offer a big benefit? ☐ ☐

   Suggested Improvement: _____

   _____

2. Is the copy easy to see and read? ☐ ☐

   Suggested Improvement: _____

   _____

3. Have you established audience identity so it is easy for the readers to see themselves in and involved by the advertising? ☐ ☐

   Suggested Improvement: _____

   _____

4. Does the copy attract the audience by being new? ☐ ☐

   Suggested Improvement: _____

   _____

5. Is the copy believable? ☐ ☐

   Suggested Improvement: _____

   _____

6. Has the copy stressed what is unique? ☐ ☐

   Suggested Improvement: _____

   _____

Source: *Which Ad Pulled Best?* by Philip Ward Burton and Scott C. Purvis (1986)

Guidelines for Creating TV Commercials That Sell

Every day, the average American spends more hours with television than with any other medium. At the same time, advertisers are faced with rapidly escalating television costs and consumers who can "Zap" out and "Zip" through their commercials. *Guidelines for Creating TV Commercials That Sell* will help you develop commercials that will rack up sales—not just creative awards.

	YES	NO

1. Have you done your basic research first and gathered all the facts on your product or service *and* the competition? ☐ ☐

   Suggested Improvement: _____

   _____

2. Have you emphasized your main selling point—your single, strongest, most provocative idea? ☐ ☐

   Suggested Improvement: _____

   _____

3. Have you made your commercial relevant to your viewers' wants and needs and respected their sensitivities and intelligence? ☐ ☐

   Suggested Improvement: _____

   _____

4. Have you "interrupted" the consumer and gotten his or her attention fast—and kept it? ☐ ☐

   Suggested Improvement: _____

   _____

5. Have you let the viewer know "What's in it for me?" ☐ ☐

   Suggested Improvement: _____

   _____

YES   NO

6. Have you matched the format, structure and style of your commercial so they are all compatible with each other and with your product or service? ☐   ☐

   Suggested Improvement: _____

   _____

7. Have you matched the video with the audio so as not to confuse the viewer? ☐   ☐

   Suggested Improvement: _____

   _____

8. Are you on track with your strategy statement and marketing objectives? Do you clearly demonstrate the benefits of the product or service? ☐   ☐

   Suggested Improvement: _____

   _____

9. Have you avoided wasting words since television is primarily a visual medium? ☐   ☐

   Suggested Improvement: _____

   _____

10. Have you kept your commercial simple and avoided cramming your spot with too many scenes, too much action or too many effects? ☐   ☐

    Suggested Improvement: _____

    _____

11. Have you written clearly and conversationally? ☐   ☐

    Suggested Improvement: _____

    _____

12. Have you clearly identified your product or service and implanted the brand name strongly in the viewer's mind? ☐   ☐

    Suggested Improvement: _____

    _____

Creating TV Commercials That Sell

13. Have you timed your commercial to make sure it is not so fast that it loses its dramatic appeal and leaves the viewer behind?　☐　☐

    Suggested Improvement: _____

    _____

14. Have you treated news as news if your product is new or has a new feature?　☐　☐

    Suggested Improvement: _____

    _____

15. Have you repeated yourself to help register your selling idea?　☐　☐

    Suggested Improvement: _____

    _____

16. Have you concentrated on writing and not on drawing?　☐　☐

    Suggested Improvement: _____

    _____

17. Are you prepared to revise, revise, revise?　☐　☐

    Suggested Improvement: _____

    _____

18. Have (or will) you give some free rein to the producer to make the commercial even better?　☐　☐

    Suggested Improvement: _____

    _____

Source: *The Radio & Television Commercial*, by Albert C. Book, Norman D. Cary and Stanley I. Tannenbaum (1984)

A Last Minute Checkup on Your TV Storyboard

Speak now or forever hold your peace! That's how every commercial producer feels before shooting starts. And just as an automobile needs a careful inspection prior to a long trip, the TV storyboard needs a final checkup before production begins. A thorough checkup will save you time and money—and can mean the difference between great success and dismal failure in the final product.

	YES	NO
1. Is there a single central message or idea?	☐	☐

Action to Take: _____

_____

2. Is the message you want to communicate clearly and explicitly stated?   ☐   ☐

Action to Take: _____

_____

3. Can you communicate the actions you want in the desired atmosphere within the time available?   ☐   ☐

Action to Take: _____

_____

4. Does the opening shot set the stage and convey only what is essential to the understanding of what follows?   ☐   ☐

Action to Take: _____

_____

5. Do the opening seconds involve the viewer and attract his attention in a way that is relevant to him and the product?   ☐   ☐

Action to Take: _____

_____

A Checkup on Your TV Storyboard

YES   NO

6. Do the shots progress in a "logical" order (or "illogically logical" order) and does each successive shot advance the story and add to the viewer's knowledge of what is going on?   ☐   ☐

    Action to Take: _____

    _____

7. Are the pictures explicit, simple and single-minded?   ☐   ☐

    Action to Take: _____

    _____

8. Do the words reinforce the pictures or are they merely redundant?   ☐   ☐

    Action to Take: _____

    _____

9. Are "supers" in sync with the audio so that they say the same thing at the same time?   ☐   ☐

    Action to Take: _____

    _____

10. Are the words clear and meaningful *in themselves* and will they be understood by a majority of the viewers?   ☐   ☐

    Action to Take: _____

    _____

11. Are the words clear and meaningful at each point in the story or do they depend for their meaning or impact on something that has not yet occurred in the story?   ☐   ☐

    Action to Take: _____

    _____

A Checkup on Your TV Storyboard

YES   NO

12. Is the copy structured to maximize the impact of the visuals?   ☐   ☐

    Action to Take: _____

    _____

13. Could the viewer repeat the story of the commercial without mentioning the product (so it seems as if the product came out of left field and the story is an irrelevant attention getter)?   ☐   ☐

    Action to Take: _____

    _____

14. Does the product enter at the *right moment* and not just at the first moment?   ☐   ☐

    Action to Take: _____

    _____

15. If it is a :60, could you cut it to a :30 (or if a :30, could it be cut to a :15)? The point is...how much does the extra time really add to the idea?   ☐   ☐

    Action to Take: _____

    _____

16. Is the commercial story believable? If no, is the selling message believable within the unbelievable or exaggerated story?   ☐   ☐

    Action to Take: _____

    _____

Source: *Creating Effective TV Commercials,* by Huntley Baldwin (1982)

17

Guidelines for Creating Radio Commercials That Sell

Radio is everywhere. It is in the home, in the car, on the beach. It rests on the teen's shoulder and it is stuck in the jogger's ear. Today, radio is even piped into the supermarket providing the closest-to-purchase exposure of any advertising medium. Refer to *Guidelines for Creating Radio Commercials That Sell* before you start writing, refer to it as you write, and then use it for one final checkup before you go into production.

	YES	NO
1. Have you written conversationally for the ear so that the commercial is *visually* and *conceptually* clear through words and sounds?	☐	☐

Suggested Improvements: _____

_____

2. Have you involved the listener and captured and excited his or her imagination?	☐	☐

Suggested Improvements: _____

_____

3. Did you stick to one strong, central idea?	☐	☐

Suggested Improvements: _____

_____

4. Have you singled out your prospect and written just to him or her?	☐	☐

Suggested Improvements: _____

_____

5. Does the commercial sound the way your prospect speaks?	☐	☐

Suggested Improvements: _____

_____

Creating Radio Commercials That Sell

	YES	NO

6. Did you set the mood for your product based upon *how* you want the listener to hear and react? ☐ ☐

Suggested Improvements: _____

_____

7. Have you remembered your mnemonics—those words, music and effects that can register in your prospect's mind? ☐ ☐

Suggested Improvements: _____

_____

8. Have you gotten attention fast? ☐ ☐

Suggested Improvements: _____

_____

9. Is the brand clearly identified and will the product's name be quickly and easily registered in the consumer's mind? ☐ ☐

Suggested Improvements: _____

_____

10. Have you avoided overwriting and crowding your spot with too much copy? ☐ ☐

Suggested Improvements: _____

_____

11. Have you made your appeal clear? ☐ ☐

Suggested Improvements: _____

_____

Creating Radio Commercials That Sell

	YES	NO

12. If your message is news, have you made it sound important? ☐ ☐

    Suggested Improvements: _____

    _____

13. Have you kept a friendly feeling throughout your message? ☐ ☐

    Suggested Improvements: _____

    _____

14. If your spot is supposed to be humorous, is it really funny? ☐ ☐

    Suggested Improvements: _____

    _____

15. Have you considered multiplying your television impressions by using your TV audio in your radio spot? ☐ ☐

    Suggested Improvements: _____

    _____

16. Have you given your listener something to do—to react to your message, to remember it, to act upon it? ☐ ☐

    Suggested Improvements: _____

    _____

17. Once is not enough, so have you repeated anything the listener might not get the first (or second) time? ☐ ☐

    Suggested Improvements: _____

    _____

Source: *The Radio & Television Commercial*, by Albert C. Book, Norman D. Cary and Stanley I. Tannenbaum (1984)

The Local Advertising
Idea-Starter Kit

With limited financial resources, the local advertiser must continually rely on his own imagination for the creation of effective selling concepts. Sometimes, the most difficult task is coming up with that first idea. *The Local Advertising Idea-Starter Kit* includes 104 ideas covering 42 product and service categories. The challenge is the "blank space" in which you should add your own creativity.

Air Conditioning and Heating Companies

Home Insulation and Energy Conservation _____

_____

_____

_____

Airlines

Exercises for the Business Traveler _____

Great Restaurants around the Country (World) _____

Getting Ready for Your Vacation _____

_____

_____

_____

Appliance Stores

Household Safety Tips _____

Energy Saving Tips _____

_____

_____

_____

Art Galleries and Dealers

What to Look for in Buying Art _____

_____

_____

_____

The Local Advertising Idea-Starter Kit

Automobile Dealers

Where to Go and How to Get There _____

How to Shop for a Car _____

_____

_____

_____

Automobile Supply Stores

Do-It-Yourself Video Car Manual _____

_____

_____

_____

Bakeries

Entertaining for the Holidays _____

Tips on Party Planning _____

_____

_____

_____

Banks and Savings and Loans

Personal Finance _____

The ABC's of Getting a Loan _____

The ABC's of the IRA _____

_____

_____

_____

Bedding Companies

Interpreting Your Dreams _____

_____

_____

_____

The Local Advertising Idea-Starter Kit

Boats and Marine Equipment

Boating Conditions in Your Area _____

Tips on Sailing _____

_____

_____

_____

Bookstores

Book Review of the Week _____

The Top 10 Books of the Week _____

_____

_____

_____

Building Material

How to Build Almost Anything _____

What to Keep in Your Garage _____

_____

_____

_____

Burglar Alarms and Security Systems

Safeguarding Your Valuables _____

Protecting Your Home against Intruders _____

_____

_____

_____

The Local Advertising Idea-Starter Kit

Clothing Stores

Community Fashion Shows _____

The Latest Fashions _____

Clothes for the Working Woman _____

How to Coordinate and Care for Your Wardrobe _____

_____

_____

_____

Cosmetics and Beauty Aids

Make-up and Beauty Hints _____

Taking Care of Your Face, Feet and Hands _____

_____

_____

_____

Dental and Medical Services

Exercises at Your Desk _____

Foods for a Healthier You _____

Taking Care of Your Mind and Body _____

Kick the Smoking Habit _____

_____

_____

_____

Drugstores

Organizing Your Medicine Cabinet _____

Lists to Leave for the Babysitter _____

_____

_____

_____

The Local Advertising Idea-Starter Kit

Educational Institutions

Going Back to School after 30! _____

_____

_____

_____

Employment and Recruitment Agencies

How to Interview for a Job _____

Assessing Your Strengths and Weaknesses _____

Writing an Effective Resume _____

_____

_____

_____

Financial Services

Tips on Keeping Tax Records _____

Understanding the New Tax Laws _____

Tax Deductions You May Have Overlooked _____

The Stock Market Report _____

Planning the Family Budget _____

_____

_____

_____

Furniture Stores

Caring for Your Furniture _____

Arranging Furniture in Your Home _____

Interior Decorating on a Budget _____

_____

_____

_____

The Local Advertising Idea-Starter Kit

**Garden and
Lawn Supplies**

Planning Your Summer Garden _____

Caring for Your Garden _____

Loving Your Plants _____

New and Different Salads _____

_____

_____

_____

Grocery Stores

Holiday Food Ideas _____

Meals on a Budget _____

Recipes for the Working Woman _____

How to Fix a Last-Minute Dinner _____

Planning Your Shopping List _____

Summer Picnic Meals _____

Seasonal Food Specialties _____

_____

_____

_____

**Hardware
Dealers**

Complete Do-It-Yourself Manual _____

How to Repair Almost Anything _____

Organizing Your Kitchen _____

Women in the Hardware Store _____

_____

_____

_____

The Local Advertising Idea-Starter Kit

Health Food Stores

Eating for a Healthier Life _____

Putting Nutrition in Your Diet _____

_____

_____

_____

Hobby Shops

Things to Do on a Rainy Day _____

Fun for the Family _____

Hobbies in Your Town _____

_____

_____

Home Improvements and Remodeling

Remodeling on a Budget _____

Redoing the Kitchen and Bath _____

_____

_____

_____

Hotels and Motels

Spending the Weekend in Town _____

Entertainment Guide of the Week _____

_____

_____

_____

Insurance Agencies

How to Buy Insurance _____

How Much Insurance Is Enough _____

_____

_____

_____

The Local Advertising Idea-Starter Kit

Luggage Stores
Packing the Most in the Least Space _____

Matching Your Luggage to Your Travel Needs _____

_____

_____

_____

Movers
Getting Ready to Move _____

Last Minute Moving Checklist _____

_____

_____

_____

Office Equipment
Buying a Personal Computer _____

Organizing Your Workspace More Efficiently _____

_____

_____

_____

Pest Control and Exterminators
The Warning Signs of Pest Danger _____

When to Call the Exterminator _____

_____

_____

_____

Photo Equipment Stores
Photography Made Easy _____

How to Photograph Children _____

Choosing the Right Camera (Film) _____

_____

_____

The Local Advertising Idea-Starter Kit

Real Estate Firms

Video Home Tours _____

Round-the-Clock Cable Home Listings _____

_____

_____

_____

Restaurants

Favorite Meals of the Chef _____

Favorites of the Celebrities _____

_____

_____

_____

Service Stations

Getting Your Car Set for Winter (or Summer) _____

Safe Driving Tips _____

When Your Car Won't Start _____

_____

_____

_____

Sporting Goods Stores

High School Sports _____

Tips for (Golf, Tennis, etc.) _____

Sportswear Fashions _____

_____

_____

_____

The Local Advertising Idea-Starter Kit

Stereos and Hi-Fi's   Video Music Show (featuring local talent) _____

How to Shop for a Stereo _____

_____

_____

_____

Theaters   Entertainment Gossip News _____

Movie Trivia Quiz _____

_____

_____

_____

Travel Agencies   Vacations on a Budget _____

Where to Go for a Weekend _____

Exotic Spots to Visit _____

_____

_____

_____

Veterinarians   Taking Care of Your Dog or Cat _____

Taking Your Pet on Vacation _____

Training Your Dog or Cat _____

_____

_____

_____

19

Should You Sponsor a Home Video?

Now that more and more people own VCRs, advertisers are actively investigating opportunities to communicate with their customers via home video. This may involve development and/or sponsorship of programming related to their product, service or corporate interests. Before investing money or time in such a venture, complete this checklist. Each question you answer "No" to represents a problem you will need to overcome if your home video venture is to be a success.

Is There a Problem?

	YES	NO
1. Does the idea offer a potentially high level of consumer interest?	☐	☐

Why? _____

_____

2. Is the home video product well conceived? Will it be well executed, and will it be compelling and exciting to view?	☐	☐

Why? _____

_____

3. Will the home video communicate better than print in a highly visual manner?	☐	☐

Why? _____

_____

4. Is there a strong distribution facility that will move the video into the home?	☐	☐

Why? _____

_____

5. Will the home video be part of an extended total merchandising package which you offer?	☐	☐

Why? _____

_____

Part III

Maneuvering through the Media

Without media, the finest ad is no more than a snapshot; the most outstanding television commercial is only a home movie. The goal of media is to effectively and efficiently deliver your advertising to your customers—and Part III's 10 checklists and charts will help you accomplish this. They focus on building and implementing a media plan based upon practical, actionable media objectives, and determining which media will best meet these objectives. A step-by-step examination of what your media plan is missing will help you develop creative new ways of using media. And you can evaluate whether the fast-growing field of event marketing would have a positive impact on your business and your customers.

20

10 Principles of Sound Media Management

Are you a sound media manager? This checklist gives you a chance to find out. Answer each question honestly. Then for each question to which you have answered *No,* indicate what you might do to change your response to *Yes.* Keep your completed self-analysis handy and refer to it often. In that way, you can monitor the degree to which you accomplish the goals of sound media management you have set for yourself.

	YES	NO
1. Are you a money manager who never forgets that the numbers in a media plan are backed by *real* dollars?	☐	☐
2. Are you careful to remember that effectiveness is primary and efficiency is not necessarily the key criterion?	☐	☐
3. Do you appreciate that all numbers are *estimates* based upon a sampling of the population, and that they can swing up or down depending on the research technique, the time of year and the particular sample chosen?	☐	☐
4. Are you creative? Do you think? Do you innovate?	☐	☐
5. Are you conversant with all media forms and do you keep on top of the latest developments?	☐	☐

Principles of Sound Media Management

6. Do you evaluate all reasonable alternatives?   ☐   ☐

_____

_____

7. Do you constantly monitor the performance of your media plan's delivery, upgrade it when possible, and correct discrepancies immediately?   ☐   ☐

_____

_____

8. Do you keep all those with whom you work informed about the latest media trends?   ☐   ☐

_____

_____

9. Have you established and do you maintain a strong rapport with media suppliers?   ☐   ☐

_____

_____

10. Are you involved in the total marketing picture rather than just with those issues involving media matters? Do you seek to recommend marketing, creative and/or new product ideas that can build your business?   ☐   ☐

_____

_____

Source: *Media Planning: A Practical Guide*, by Jim Surmanek (1985)

21

A Model for Media Planning

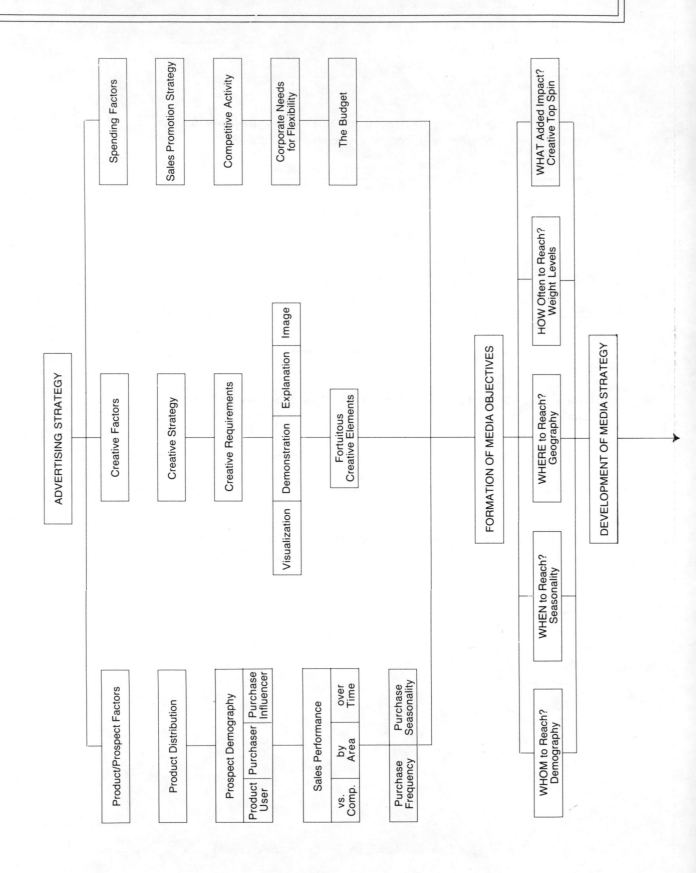

A Model for Media Planning

The media planning process begins with a thorough study of the advertising strategy. It continues by establishing a set of media objectives from which a media strategy is derived. From here, the full media plan is developed, after which the plan is implemented by buying and scheduling media time and space.

A Model for Media Planning documents this process in a flow chart.

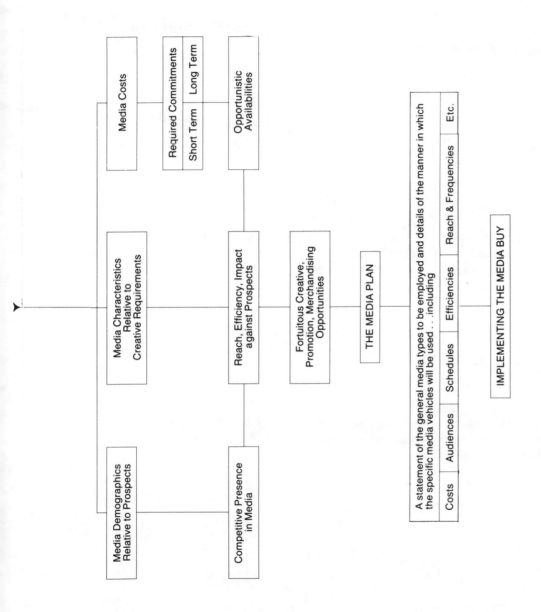

22 Checking Up on Your Media Plan

A media plan is put together with care and concern to accomplish certain objectives. The degree to which the plan succeeds depends upon whether these objectives are the correct ones, and, if so, whether the media plan successfully implements them. Use the following checklist to make certain that your media plan carries out the goals you have set for it.

	Is Our Objective on Target?	Does the Plan Implement It?

1. WHOM do we want to reach? Are we certain this is the correct target? Have we missed anyone who might be a significant product or service user, purchaser or influencer?

   Suggested Improvement: _____   ☐   ☐

   _____

   _____

2. WHEN do we want to reach them? Are we certain we are reaching them when they will not only be interested in our product or service but also be most interested in receiving our message? Have we considered not only what time of the year, but also what times of the week and what times of the day we should reach them?

   Suggested Improvement: _____   ☐   ☐

   _____

   _____

3. WHERE do we want to reach them? Are we focusing on those geographic areas where our dollars can work most productively? Has the plan considered all of the regional and local marketing factors that influence the purchase and usage of our product or service? Have we considered how our market focus will impact upon key factors in the trade?

   Suggested Improvement: _____   ☐   ☐

   _____

   _____

4. HOW MANY do we need to reach? Are we reaching enough prospects with our message during a specific promotional period or within a specific time frame that relates to our product or service's purchase or usage cycle?

   Suggested Improvement: _____   ☐   ☐

   _____

   _____

Checking Up on Your Media Plan

	Is Our Objective on Target?	Does the Plan Implement It?

5. HOW FREQUENTLY do we need to reach them? Are we reaching them often enough to make our point, yet not so often that we waste money that could more profitably be directed elsewhere?

Suggested Improvement: _____ ☐ ☐

_____

_____

6. WHAT MEDIA provide the best environments and conditions under which to reach our prospects? Have we selected media that will enhance the delivery of our message? Will it help us stand out from the crowd and the clutter?

Suggested Improvement: _____ ☐ ☐

_____

_____

7. AT WHAT COST do we reach our prospects? Are we spending too much to accomplish our objectives? Or are we spending so little that we are in essence "invisible"? Are we spending enough not only in total but also in each individual medium vehicle so as to establish an effective presence? Have we considered not only the present activity of our competition, but also their anticipated future activity?

Suggested Improvement: _____ ☐ ☐

_____

_____

8. IS ANYTHING MISSING. . .OR SHOULD ANYTHING BE DONE DIFFERENTLY? Have we looked at our media plan from all angles? Have we challenged it? Have we compared it with other reasonable alternatives?

Suggested Improvement: _____ ☐ ☐

_____

_____

The Media Value Checklist

Every medium has certain distinct characteristics that contribute to (or detract from) the effective and efficient communication of advertising to the consumer. Noted in *The Media Value Checklist* is whether each of these characteristics tends to be a positive or a negative force. In the adjacent boxes, check those points which are of significance to you. The results of your media appraisal will help you determine whether or not a given medium should be included in your media mix.

	+ Force	– Force	Significance to Me
TELEVISION			
Intrusive	X		☐
Impactful with sight, sound, movement	X		☐
Highly merchandiseable to the trade	X		☐
National-network and local-spot flexibility	X		☐
Sponsorship/program control potential	X		☐
Immediate broad reach potential across many target audiences	X		☐
High frequency potential in selected dayparts (day, late night)	X		☐
Opportunities to flight or pulse in line with budget and product potential	X		☐
Increasing concern with clutter and zapping		X	☐
High absolute costs for network		X	☐
Subject to sudden price escalation due to laws of supply and demand		X	☐
A mass medium with less efficient delivery against narrowly defined targets		X	☐
Short-term delivery risk due to continuous programming changes		X	☐

The Media Value Checklist

	+ Force	− Force	Significance to Me
CABLE TELEVISION			
Highly selective programming to zero-in on highly selective target audiences	X		☐
Sponsorship opportunities to achieve program identity	X		☐
Upscale audiences with higher incomes, more education and larger families	X		☐
Product exclusivity	X		☐
Ability to test creative commercial ideas at low media costs	X		☐
Flexible commercial message lengths and forms	X		☐
National-network and local-spot flexibility	X		☐
Ability to tag commercials locally on some networks	X		☐
Low costs per commercial announcement	X		☐
Excellent CPMs for network cable	X		☐
Ability to build high frequency of exposure	X		☐
Opportunity to compensate for lower broadcast ratings in cable homes	X		☐
Limited national reach with cable coverage in about half of all U. S. TV homes		X	☐
Coverage deficiencies in certain markets		X	☐
Local cable buys generally expensive with high CPMs		X	☐
Proof of performance problems		X	☐
Less research than on broadcast television		X	☐

The Media Value Checklist

	+ Force	- Force	Significance to Me
RADIO			
National-network and local-spot flexibility	X		☐
"Theater of the Mind" using listener's imagination	X		☐
Wide variety of formats and personalities for targeted exposure to specific demographic segments	X		☐
Enhances a television campaign with audio "imagery transfer"	X		☐
Strong merchandising from networks and local stations	X		☐
Significant local market identification	X		☐
Ability to build high frequency of exposure	X		☐
Good reach potential through multiple station buys	X		☐
Reaches mobile audience often at point nearest purchase	X		☐
High summer listening when TV viewing is lowest	X		☐
Low costs per commercial announcement	X		☐
Excellent CPMs	X		☐
Often used as a background medium for other activities		X	☐
Limited to single audio dimension		X	☐
Clutter with as many as 18 commercial minutes per hour		X	☐
High cost for broad reach due to audience fragmentation		X	☐
30-second commercials priced expensively relative to 60s		X	☐

The Media Value Checklist

	+ Force	- Force	Significance to Me
MAGAZINES			
Significant audience selectivity against various demographic and psychographic groups	X		☐
Compatible editorial environment	X		☐
Long life with opportunity for repeat exposure	X		☐
Opportunity for longer reader exposure to ad message	X		☐
Excellent color reproduction	X		☐
Creative opportunities with a variety of different space units	X		☐
Wide geographic and demographic flexibility	X		☐
Broad reach potential through use of large circulation magazines and/or a variety of different category books	X		☐
Strong reach among upscale targets	X		☐
Builds audience among light TV viewers	X		☐
Good overall CPMs when pass-along audience is included	X		☐
Excellent efficiencies relative to other media among very selective, upscale targets	X		☐
Non-intrusive relative to broadcast since reader self-selects subject matter		X	☐
Growing clutter in ad banks and low editorial ratios in certain magazines		X	☐
Single visual dimension only		X	☐
Moderate to low frequency builder		X	☐
Generally below-average delivery in the South and parts of the West (partly a function of demographics in these areas)		X	☐
Continuing question of print communication value relative to television		X	☐
High regional and metro rate premiums		X	☐
Uncertainties created with rate negotiating		X	☐

The Media Value Checklist

	+ Force	− Force	Significance to Me
NEWSPAPERS			
Immediate, announcement value in newsworthy environment	X		☐
Benefits from established reader habits	X		☐
Opportunity for long copy, shopping perusal	X		☐
Special-interest targeting potential in specific sections and papers (college, ethnic)	X		☐
Geographic targeting	X		☐
Merchandiseable to local dealers	X		☐
High local market penetration and identity	X		☐
Growing variety of space units	X		☐
Strong coop opportunities, with local retail support	X		☐
Short lifespan, with little repeat exposure opportunities		X	☐
Retail ad clutter with little competitive separation		X	☐
Predominantly primary readership with limited secondary or pass-along readers		X	☐
Unreliable (but improving) ROP color reproduction		X	☐
Declining readership among younger adults, and in suburban areas		X	☐
High cost of running multi-market campaign		X	☐
High CPMs except for small space units		X	☐
Difficult to attain true national coverage due to concentration in major urban areas		X	☐
Mass penetration allows little audience selectivity		X	☐
Limited negotiability		X	☐
Premiums for special positions		X	☐
Significant premiums for national vs. local advertisers		X	☐

The Media Value Checklist

	+ Force	– Force	Significance to Me
SUNDAY SUPPLEMENTS			
High local market coverage due to newspaper carrier penetration	X		☐
In-home, relaxed readership	X		☐
Good color reproduction	X		☐
Highly merchandiseable	X		☐
Broad reach potential	X		☐
Local market impact with a magazine format	X		☐
Little secondary or pass-along audience		X	☐
Not a considered purchase, like magazines		X	☐
Limited audience selectivity due to means of distribution		X	☐
High out-of-pocket cost and CPM for national coverage		X	☐
OUT-OF-HOME			
Excellent reminder medium supporting other vehicles	X		☐
24-hour exposure	X		☐
Opportunity for strong package and product identification	X		☐
Graphic flexibility	X		☐
Strong local market presence	X		☐
Broad reach and high frequency potential	X		☐
Impact of large space units	X		☐
Opportunity to rotate locations to maximize audience delivery	X		☐
Positioning opportunities near the point of purchase	X		☐
Excellent CPMs	X		☐
Limited to short, simple message		X	☐

The Media Value Checklist

	+ Force	- Force	Significance to Me
Demographic selectivity difficult, although not impossible		X	☐
Increasingly restricted availabilities due to zoning laws		X	☐
High out-of-pocket costs for multi-market coverage		X	☐

DIRECT MAIL

	+ Force	- Force	Significance to Me
High degree of demographic, geographic and "buying behavior" selectivity depending upon mailing list used	X		☐
Wide variety of sizes, shapes and forms	X		☐
Intrusive	X		☐
Numerous response options	X		☐
Flexible	X		☐
Excellent reproduction	X		☐
High reach potential against selected targets	X		☐
Ability to build frequency through multiple mailings	X		☐
Timing not subject to media availability	X		☐
Reaches target at home or at work	X		☐
Efficient if target is hard to reach with mass media	X		☐
Not a requested or purchased medium by the consumer and must stand on its own for recognition		X	☐
Often regarded as "junk mail"		X	☐
A short life, unless of real interest to the consumer		X	☐
High cost and CPM for mass distribution		X	☐
Impacted by postal regulations		X	☐

Implementing a Media Buy

The implementation of a sound media buy should follow a well-organized, step-by-step procedure.

First, you must examine your overall media communications requirements as documented in the media plan. These will help you determine how well each media opportunity can accomplish your objectives.

Next, you will evaluate and negotiate specific media proposals.

In the third stage, a decision to buy is made. That is the time to send out order letters, handle the trafficking of advertising materials and wrap up all publicity and promotion efforts surrounding the purchase.

Once the buy has been made and the advertising begins to run, you will evaluate audience response, prepare stewardship reports, and handle billing and payment. At the same time, you will continue to explore future media opportunities.

Implementing a Media Buy is shown below in a flow chart.

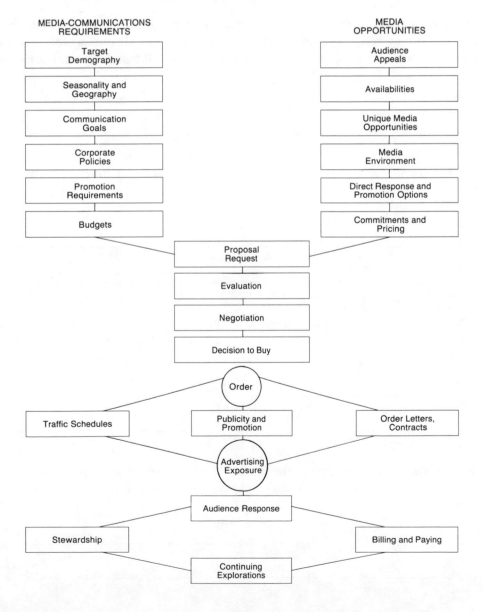

Guiding the Search
for a Creative Media Concept

In an ever-changing advertising environment, marketers must constantly seek out new ways to reach their customers with maximum communications effectiveness. Using this creative media concept questionnaire as a guide, ask yourself each of the following questions. Your answers will help you explore new media options as you develop future advertising plans and media strategies.

1. How can a creative concept in one medium "precondition" an audience to receive a message that follows it in another medium in order that this latter exposure can work harder? (Example: A magazine or newspaper ad that promotes your new television commercials)

_____

_____

2. How can a creative media concept provide a synergistic editorial and advertising bond, help to attract the consumer to your message, and even hold the reader's eyes on your message for important added seconds? (Example: An ad for baby food placed next to an editorial feature on caring for infants)

_____

_____

3. How can a creative media concept deliver multiple exposures of a single insertion at no added cost? (Example: An ad continued from one page to the next that results in the reader flipping back and forth to get the full effect of the message)

_____

_____

4. How can a creative media concept deliver a dominant presence in a medium and position a company or brand as dominant in the industry? (Example: A "live" outdoor billboard in front of which performers demonstrate a product)

_____

_____

5. How can a creative media concept deliver the impact of a larger space unit, but at less cost than for the larger unit? (Example: A "checkerboard" magazine spread with editorial material interspersed between the advertising)

_____

_____

The Search for a Creative Media Concept

6. How can a single "blockbuster" creative media concept set you apart from the competition? (Example: A "pop-up" magazine ad)

   _____

   _____

7. How can a creative media concept make the consumer actually seek out your advertising? (Example: Delivering a crossword puzzle to the consumer as part of your ad)

   _____

   _____

8. How can a creative media concept add believability and authenticity to a product or brand story? (Example: A television commercial for a new fast-start lawn mower in which the mower is actually started live on television)

   _____

   _____

9. How can a single creative media concept provide the sole basis for a brand or company's advertising effort and provide exceptional public relations "topspin"? (Example: A music video created by an advertiser that incorporates the product into the message and is run on MTV)

   _____

   _____

10. How can a creative media concept deliver a sales promotion effort in a new or unique environment? (Example: A video or an audio "coupon" in which the commercial tells the viewers or listeners how they can make their own money-saving coupon)

    _____

    _____

11. How can a creative media concept deliver a message that is too involved, complex or unusual to deliver through traditional media channels? (Example: A home video designed to show the product or service in an environment that will encourage viewing)

    _____

    _____

12. How can a creative media concept be delivered to the consumer when he or she is shopping or participating in an activity related to your product? (Example: Advertising on shopping bags)

_____

_____

13. How can a creative media concept provide you with exposure in an environment where your competition dominates everything around you? (Example: "Sponsoring" the sports scores in the newspaper if your competition actually sponsors all of the sports on television)

_____

_____

14. Anything else?

_____

_____

26

The Creative Media
Pocket Planner

A portable organizer designed to stimulate innovation and the development of creative media ideas in and out of meetings . . . on airplanes and commuter trains . . . at the beach or out in the yard . . . anywhere by anyone at anytime.

The Product or Service

1. What consumer response do I want my advertising to produce?

_____

_____

_____

2. What traditional media approaches can help deliver this response?

_____

_____

_____

3. What media will my customers expect me to use?

_____

_____

_____

4. What media do I expect my competition to use?

_____

_____

_____

5. What seems to be missing from my media plan?

_____

_____

_____

6. What creative media concepts can I relate to my customers and . . .

Who they are? _____

_____

How they use my product or service? _____

_____

Where they use it? _____

_____

When they use it? _____

_____

7. What unique media twist that I have always wanted to try might work?

_____

_____

_____

8. Could I create a media blockbuster and extend it over time and across different media?

_____

_____

_____

The Creative Media Pocket Planner

SAMPLE CREATIVE MEDIA IDEA STARTERS

- ☐ Roadblocking (Commercials opposite each other)
- ☐ Gridlocking (Commercials opposite, before and after each other)
- ☐ Program sponsorship
- ☐ Announcing one media event in another medium
- ☐ Season, day or time tie-ins
- ☐ Multiple messages in a row (the Burma Shave Effect)
- ☐ Matched multimedia synergy (Business magazines plus business television)
- ☐ The live event
- ☐ Readership-enhancing editorial adjacencies
- ☐ Related program environment (the Weather Channel and snow tires)
- ☐ Infomercials
- ☐ Polling with the telephone
- ☐ MiniQuiz (Commercials between question and answer)
- ☐ Cross-media promotions
- ☐ Commercial tags with offers
- ☐ Multiple small space ads
- ☐ New magazine premiere issues
- ☐ Exclusive magazine special-issue sponsorships
- ☐ Sponsored videocassettes
- ☐ Product videos (also MTV music videos)
- ☐ Pop-up ads
- ☐ Electronic talking and flashing ads
- ☐ Scented ads
- ☐ Unusual sizes and shapes
- ☐ Tie-ins with major events
- ☐ Tie-ins with natural phenomena
- ☐ Public relations tie-ins
- ☐ Direct marketing tie-ins

27

How to Evaluate TV Special Sponsorship Opportunities

To stand out in an increasingly cluttered advertising environment, companies may seek opportunities in television program sponsorship. Since high risks and large dollar commitments are associated with sponsoring a television special, a decision to sponsor must be carefully considered. This checklist will guide you in evaluating sponsorship opportunities in light of a company's overall marketing and advertising objectives.

	YES	NO
1. Will the special reach your target audience?	☐	☐

Why not? _____

_____

2. Will the program content be compatible with your overall advertising objectives and corporate policies?   ☐ ☐

Why not? _____

_____

3. Will the program environment enhance the delivery of your corporate and/or product commercials?   ☐ ☐

Why not? _____

_____

4. Does it have the potential to deliver an audience size commensurate with the cost of sponsorship?   ☐ ☐

Why not? _____

_____

5. Can it be regarded as a major television event that will truly stand out from regular television programming?   ☐ ☐

Why not? _____

_____

6. Can it be effectively promoted to potential viewers and to the trade?   ☐ ☐

Why not? _____

_____

TV Sponsorship Opportunities

	YES	NO

7. Can you benefit from being in a sheltered or controlled environment away from your competition and other advertisers?   ☐ ☐

   Why not? _____

   _____

8. Is the program idea fresh, innovative and different? Will it let you stand out from the crowd of other advertisers?   ☐ ☐

   Why not? _____

   _____

9. Do the production staff and talent have strong credentials?   ☐ ☐

   Why not? _____

   _____

10. Will all aspects of the show be handled with good taste?   ☐ ☐

   Why not? _____

   _____

11. Does the special have the potential to generate strong, positive publicity and earn awards?   ☐ ☐

   Why not? _____

   _____

12. Can you anticipate receiving strong, positive viewer response?   ☐ ☐

   Why not? _____

   _____

13. Are there merchandising and promotion opportunities that can be easily, effectively and efficiently exploited?   ☐ ☐

   Why not? _____

   _____

TV Sponsorship Opportunities

	YES	NO

14. Can you benefit from utilizing variable length commercials, including 90-second and 2-minute messages? ☐ ☐

    Why not? _____

    _____

15. Will you have flexibility in what you choose to say in the opening and closing billboards? ☐ ☐

    Why not? _____

    _____

16. Does the special have long-term "evergreen" potential? Could you be associated with it annually? ☐ ☐

    Why not? _____

    _____

17. Will the special serve as a focal point for a thematically integrated advertising, promotion and public relations effort? ☐ ☐

    Why not? _____

    _____

18. Is the special the best of potential alternatives? ☐ ☐

    Why not? _____

    _____

19. Will your investment in a special be more productive than spending the same dollars on other marketing activities? ☐ ☐

    Why not? _____

    _____

28 Questions to Ask When Considering Sponsorship of an Event

A growing number of advertisers have shifted traditional media dollars into event marketing. Used properly, the sponsorship of an event can have a very positive effect on your customers, the trade and your own employees. Its value can even extend to influencing educators, community leaders, government and many other publics. The event must "pay out" for you, however. Consider the 18 points on this checklist when evaluating an event marketing program.

	YES	NO
1. Will the event relate to your product or service's communications and selling strategies?	☐	☐

Why not? _____

_____

_____

| 2. Will it be integrated into your company's overall marketing efforts? | ☐ | ☐ |

Why not? _____

_____

_____

| 3. Is the sponsorship tied into a major promotion? Will it provide a "hook" for a more effective promotion? | ☐ | ☐ |

Why not? _____

_____

_____

| 4. Can the event also generate added trade and sales force support and enthusiasm? | ☐ | ☐ |

Why not? _____

_____

_____

Considering Sponsorship of an Event

5. Will the event attract interest among your prime prospects, or among a segment of potential prospects or purchase influencers otherwise hard to reach?　☐　☐

   Why not? _____

   _____

   _____

6. Does the event have a reasonable chance of being a "hit"? Is it a fresh idea, or is it old and tired?　☐　☐

   Why not? _____

   _____

   _____

7. Does the event offer strong public relations values?　☐　☐

   Why not? _____

   _____

   _____

8. Will the event offer you extended promotion opportunities over time, and from year to year?　☐　☐

   Why not? _____

   _____

   _____

9. Will the sponsorship provide you with an extensive presence at the event itself? with on-site signage? company identification on the participants themselves? products on-site?　☐　☐

   Why not? _____

   _____

   _____

Considering Sponsorship of an Event

	YES	NO

10. Will the event be broadcast on radio, TV, cable so that advertising can be tied to the sponsorship? ☐ ☐

Why not? _____

_____

_____

11. Can the impact of your sponsorship be enhanced by related paid media advertising? ☐ ☐

Why not? _____

_____

_____

12. Will you be able to tie in local events with a major national event? ☐ ☐

Why not? _____

_____

_____

13. Would the dollars accomplish more if you simply spent additional money on media advertising? ☐ ☐

Why not? _____

_____

_____

14. Will the event let you stand out from your competition? ☐ ☐

Why not? _____

_____

_____

15. Will you be able to get along well with "partners" who co-sponsor the event? ☐ ☐

Why not? _____

_____

_____

Considering Sponsorship of an Event

16. If you decide to bow out of the sponsorship after a few years, will you be able to do so without any embarrassing publicity in the media? ☐   ☐

    Why not? _____

    _____

    _____

17. Can the event succeed for you without excessive time and effort by your staff? ☐   ☐

    Why not? _____

    _____

    _____

18. Do you have a plan for evaluating the event's performance? ☐   ☐

    Why not? _____

    _____

    _____

Methods for Evaluating Event Sponsorship

I. Media Coverage

    A. Amount of Coverage

    B. Type of Coverage

        1. Prospect targeted vs. general audience
        2. Visibility of company identity in coverage

II. Pre- and Post-Sponsorship Surveys

    A. Sponsor and/or Product Recall

    B. Attitude Change

    C. Image

III. Actual Response Delivered

    A. Leads

    B. Sales

    C. Trade Support

A 151-Item Checklist for Conferences and Special Events

"For want of a nail, the shoe was lost. For want of a shoe, the horse was lost. For want of a horse, the message was lost. For want of a message, the battle was lost." Anyone who has ever organized or planned a meeting would agree, "For want of a projection bulb, coffee, or a nonsmoking section, the meeting was lost!" Robert Roth's Checklist covers 151 "forget-me-nots" essential to the success of any major gathering.

Starting Checklist

☐ 1. Recruit help

☐ 2. Appoint committee chairpersons for:
☐   Site selection
☐   Agenda
☐   Delegates
☐   Finance
☐   Transportation
☐   Registration

☐   Banquet
☐   Entertainment
☐   After-hours activities

☐ 3. Firm up choice of hotel

☐ 4. Arrange for monthly progress reports

☐ 5. Final report three months before meeting/seminar/convention

Accommodations Checklist

☐ 1. Total of rooms needed:
☐   Singles
☐   Doubles
☐   Suites

☐ 2. Room rates

☐ 3. Roll-away beds for children

☐ 4. Reservations to be confirmed by hotel

☐ 5. Date majority arriving

☐ 6. Check-in time limits

☐ 7. Date majority departing

☐ 8. Check-out time

☐ 9. Special VIP arrangements

☐ 10. Hospitality areas

☐ 11. Nonalcoholic hospitality suites

☐ 12. Parking garage facilities

☐ 13. Food plan
☐   AP (American Plan)
☐   MAP (Modified American Plan)
☐   European Plan

☐ 14. Credit arrangements agreed for guests

Registration Checklist

☐ 1. Procedure for guests

☐ 2. Procedure for VIPs

☐ 3. Welcoming service

☐ 4. Signs for registration desk

☐ 5. Lobby registration table if required

☐ 6. Identification badges

☐ 7. Wastebaskets

☐ 8. Hospitality rooms

☐ 9. Emergency spare rooms

☐ 10. Facilities guide

☐ 11. Agenda displayed

☐ 12. Consult hotel credit manager

☐ 13. Experts to handle money

☐ 14. Literature distributed

☐ 15. Checklists to committee members

Checklist for Conferences and Special Events

Speakers Checklist

☐ 1. Arrangements made well before meeting
☐ 2. Time speaker to be available
☐ 3. Place speaker to be available
☐ 4. Length of talk
☐ 5. Type of talk planned
☐ 6. Fee fixed
☐ 7. Expenses arranged including transportation
☐ 8. Biographical notes for introduction
☐ 9. Photograph for literature and publicity

☐ 10. Hospitality for spouse
☐ 11. Hotel reservation(s) made
☐ 12. Special equipment provided
☐ 13. Program supplied to speaker
☐ 14. Special guest(s) to be invited
☐ 15. Speaker to be met at airport/station
☐ 16. Introduced to officers, VIPs
☐ 17. Alternative speaker available
☐ 18. Flowers, refreshments, fruit in room

Bird Dog Checklist

☐ 1. Set up agenda
☐ 2. Set up daily routines
☐ 3. Arrangements made with hotel
☐ 4. All telephone numbers noted
☐ 5. All times noted

☐ 6. Literature for distribution
☐ 7. Welcoming arrangements made
☐ 8. Get-acquainted party
☐ 9. Formal welcoming speech

Meeting Rooms Checklist

☐ 1. Sufficient seats
☐ 2. . . . properly arranged
☐ 3. Place cards correct
☐ 4. Pads, pencils distributed
☐ 5. . . . and ash trays; glasses, water pitchers
☐ 6. Nonsmoking section
☐ 7. Light switches located and in working order
☐ 8. Cooling, heating controls located and checked
☐ 9. Stage equipment checked
☐ 10. Lectern ready, light working, gavel in place
☐ 11. All arrangements made for speakers
☐ 12. Speaker's pointer handy
☐ 13. Microphone checked
☐ 14. Loudspeaker in place

☐ 15. Volume adjusted
☐ 16. Extension cord no hazard
☐ 17. Easel, markers ready
☐ 18. Projection screen installed
☐ 19. Projection equipment plugged in
☐ 20. Projection lamp tested
☐ 21. Screen correct size
☐ 22. Screen correctly positioned
☐ 23. Audience view unobstructed
☐ 24. Spare lamps and fuses ready
☐ 25. Lenses clean
☐ 26. Directional signs posted
☐ 27. Rest rooms indicated
☐ 28. Member of your staff at door if necessary
☐ 29. Room(s) booked for guest speaker(s)

Checklist for Conferences and Special Events

Visual Aids Checklist

Choose among:

☐ 1. Easel pad and felt markers

☐ 2. Overhead projector

☐ 3. Slide presentation

☐ 4. Movie and video equipment

☐ 5. Closed-circuit television

Also:

☐ 6. Check projection screen size

Coffee/Cocktails Checklist

☐ 1. Place to serve coffee

☐ 2. Check coffee arrangement

☐ 3. Supply decaffeinated coffee

☐ 4. Sugar substitutes

☐ 5. Tea

☐ 6. Soft drinks

☐ 7. Arrangements to close bar

☐ 8. Appoint one person only who can keep bar open

Banquet Checklist

☐ 1. Seating arrangements

☐ 2. Speeches kept short by agreement

☐ 3. Plan menu with banquet sales manager

☐ 4. Wines—to serve or not to serve

☐ 5. Champagne—yes or no

☐ 6. Spectacular dishes—yes or no

Day-to-Day Meals Checklist

☐ 1. Check menus

☐ 2. Consult hotel's food and beverage manager

☐ 3. . . .or banquet manager

☐ 4. . . .or maitre d'hotel

☐ 5. Breakfast—buffet-style

☐ 6. Lunch—light, especially dessert

☐ 7. All meals—varied with alternative choices

Entertainment Checklist

☐ 1. Check budget. . .

☐ 2. . . .allow for emergencies

☐ 3. Professional entertainers only

☐ 4. Seek local talent

☐ 5. Show to suit audience

☐ 6. Family routine or nightclub

☐ 7. Dressing room(s) for artist(s)

☐ 8. Union regulations followed

☐ 9. Arrangements for payment

☐ 10. Arrangements for standby

☐ 11. Arrangements for artist payments

Checklist for Conferences and Special Events

After-Hours Checklist

☐ 1. Plan for pocket and purse

☐ 2. Stagger meeting hours for fun

☐ 3. Plan a pre- or post-meeting tour

Spouses Checklist

☐ 1. Plan program thoroughly

☐ 2. Know general interest

☐ 3. Consider budget

☐ 4. Consider spouses' budgets

☐ 5. Spouses' hospitality suite—staffing

☐ 6. Schedule function outside hotel for variety

☐ 7. Check for group-rate savings on activities

☐ 8. Arrange guide for bus trip

☐ 9. Arrange cultural tours

☐ 10. Fashion show

☐ 11. Arrange suitable speaker for spouses-only lecture

Printed Literature Checklist

☐ 1. Pocket program

☐ 2. Program

☐ 3. List of participants

☐ 4. Menu

☐ 5. Texts of speeches

☐ 6. Texts of panel discussions

☐ 7. Spouses' program

☐ 8. Seating plan

☐ 9. Tour program

Source: *International Market Communications,* by Robert F. Roth (1982)

Public Relations, Publicity and Promotions

Properly implemented, public relations is a very effective marketing tool. It can publicize a business, its products and its services. It can enhance the value of a business's many different activities and efforts. And it can be used to deal with outside influences —government actions, the consumer or competition—which impact upon it. Public relations activities involve many different avenues of exposure. The key to its most effective implementation is knowing how appropriate each activity is under different sets of circumstances. In other words, you need to know what works best...and when. Part IV will help you find out.

6 Guidelines for Responding to a Threatened Boycott

In recent years, advertisers have received an increasing number of threats of consumer boycotts from activist groups opposed to television programs and/or magazines which they claimed contained excessive sex or violence. When threatened with a boycott, you will in most cases respond in writing to the group opposing the media environment in which your advertising appears. Refer to the following 6 guidelines and make certain to consult with your public relations counsel in drafting your response.

1. Avoid being on the defensive, apologizing, saying it was a mistake, or indicating it will never happen again.

2. Explain it has never been your company's policy to influence a medium's editorial or programming content.

3. Indicate that in a democracy, the consumer should determine the success or failure of a medium. That he or she should decide what to read, listen to or view . . . just as he or she should be free to decide for whom to vote, how to pray, where to shop, etc.

4. Comment that the program in which your commercials appeared was reviewed prior to airing and that the subject matter was felt to have been handled in good taste.

5. Emphasize that your company runs advertising in many different media vehicles which effectively reach your customers. That your advertising schedule is never meant as an endorsement or rejection of a medium's position or policies.

6. State that in a free society, a company should not be threatened for its legal exercise of the right of free speech.

17 Public Relations, Publicity and Promotional Ideas

Many public relations activities can enhance a company's marketing activities and its position in the minds of its many publics. The key is knowing which activities work best and under what conditions. Sheryl Johnston has been counseling clients on the effective use of public relations for more than 15 years. This checklist of *17 Public Relations, Publicity and Promotional Ideas* can help you choose the right public relations tool at the right time. As Sheryl says, "The main problem people have with public relations is that they should not use it when they honestly have nothing to say!"

Public Relations Activity	Appropriate for	Not Appropriate for
PUBLIC SERVICE ANNOUNCEMENT (PSA) —is an announcement which is intended to educate or benefit the consumer audience (with no commercial mentions). These may be electronically produced or submitted in written form to be read by a station announcer. They generally come in 20-, 30-, and 60-second formats (check with station for requirements). Nonprofit status is usually required.	Educational message such as health or safety information. Event announcement (as long as it was for nonprofit reasons).	Brand name announcement. (Example: You could submit a PSA from the American Dairy Association about the benefits of cheese. But you couldn't submit a PSA for the benefits of Kraft cheese.)
RADIO TRADE FOR MENTION CONTEST—a radio promotion in which the client or agency offers a prize package (such as an all-expense-paid trip, product, cash, or various other items) to a station in "exchange for mention." The rule of thumb: Contest should have listener appeal. Station should provide client with a total number of mentions equal (in air time) to the value of the prize package.	Promoting a special event, name or product.	Promoting an idea or product which has serious overtones (e.g., a piece of medical equipment, a life-threatening situation). A story or prize package that would only be of interest to a small group of people.

Public Relations and Promotional Ideas

Public Relations Activity	Appropriate for	Not Appropriate for
PRINT CONTEST— usually a recipe or essay contest in which you provide a magazine or newspaper with the editorial idea and the prize package. In exchange, they give you space and mention of the object of your promotion. (Note: Not the same as a paid space sweepstakes.)	Promoting a special event, theme, product, etc.	Situations where there is no natural editorial tie-in, or the subject is of interest to a small group of people (unless you are going to a special interest publication that is only reaching one particular audience).
MAT RELEASE—is a black and white story and sometimes photo which can be reproduced in sizes from a column to a full page. It generally contains product or client mention and is usually run as is by editors of suburban and smaller newspapers. Client pays for production and distribution.	A story that doesn't require in-depth analysis. Good for questions and answers, recipes, contest announcements, trivia quizzes, basic who-what-when-why-where news stories.	A story which requires the editor's opinion or analysis. A story that could easily get picked up on its own because of its significance.
PRESS RELEASE—a news story which relates the who-what-when-why-where to the media.	Announcing news about a company, product, idea, promotion, person or event.	Situations when there is no story to tell (e.g., a product sampling event only).
PRESS KIT—Generally includes more than one news release, sometimes a fact sheet, photographs, biographical information, etc.	A story which requires in-depth understanding from the media.	A story which is already familiar, or which is of little significance.

Public Relations and Promotional Ideas

Public Relations Activity	Appropriate for	Not Appropriate for
PRESS CONFERENCE— an event to which a selected group of media is invited to hear an announcement or watch a demonstration of major significance. (Note: In general, the media resists press conferences if they can obtain the news another way. They will only attend if a major personality is announcing something, or if a major issue is to be discussed.)	A major announcement which has an effect on, or would be of interest to consumers.	An announcement which has a small effect. Just meeting someone (with no major announcement).
A VIDEO NEWS RELEASE—a news feature which tells a short story about an issue or product which affects consumers in some way. This is distributed to television news outlets and sometimes talk shows for use on-air, as is. The client pays for the production and distribution.	A trends story. A consumer-interest story which can be told in a noncommercial way. Note: Think of it as being part of a newscast.	A totally commercial message. A piece of news which has no benefit to the audience.
AN AUDIO NEWS RELEASE OR PAID, SYNDICATED RADIO INTERVIEW—Again, a consumer interest news story. This would be distributed to radio stations for use during various parts of the day. Client pays for production and distribution.	A consumer news interest story. Note: Must be logged by the radio station as "news" or "public affairs" programming.	A totally commercial message. A piece of news which has no benefit to the audience.

Public Relations and Promotional Ideas

Public Relations Activity	Appropriate for	Not Appropriate for
ROP COLOR PAGE—A mat feature which generally includes a color photo, recipes or "how to" tips, and a story. Client or agency provides the copy, recipes, and photo. ROP service takes care of layout, production, and distribution to editors. The editor will generally use as is, with a limited amount of commercial mentions, and can choose to use his/her own byline. If copy is too commercial, they will drop out brand name. ROP color pages usually are a half to a full page and run on the front cover of the newspaper food or lifestyle section. Cost is paid for totally by client, or can be shared with another sponsor. (Typical joint sponsors would be a barbecue sauce and a barbecue grill, or a food product with a drink.)	Recipe stories on new or existing products. Feature stories with recipes or tips, brochure send-away offers. "How to" stories affecting meal preparation or lifestyles.	A story that requires no visual and would be easily picked up by editors as a straight news release. A story that doesn't relate to food or lifestyles.
SAMPLING EVENT—an event in which the client offers its product to the public. Sometimes includes the distribution of a coupon, brochure, in addition to product sample.	Encouraging trial and usage of new or existing product. Presenting an existing product in a new way, or to secure new audiences.	Media coverage (unless there is something highly unusual going on).
EXHIBIT SPACE—a space in which you exhibit or distribute a product (or information).	New product introduction. New ways of using a product. Distributing information. Giving presentations or demonstrations.	Distributing very dry information. Exhibiting an existing product with nothing new to show or tell.

Public Relations and Promotional Ideas

Public Relations Activity	Appropriate for	Not Appropriate for
MEDIA SPOKESPERSON TOUR—Offering a media spokesperson to promote your product or idea to the general public. Usually consists of a combination of print or broadcast interviews and sometimes personal appearances.	Presenting a new product or idea to the general public. Promoting a personality such as a performer, politician, author, or athlete. Crisis public relations situation (something has happened which has in some way had a negative effect on the general public). Offering send-away (how-to or informational) brochures.	Any story that is of interest to a small group of people only. Any story that is too commercial. It should, in some way, benefit the viewing, reading or listening audience. Couponing (with no story to tell).
POSTERS, BROCHURES, SIGNAGE—Posters announcing an event or idea; brochures providing consumer information; signage designed to attract attention.	Posters and signs should be used when the purpose is to attract attention without going into a great deal of detail. Brochures work best when they can be easily distributed free of charge (e.g., at an event, through a P.O. Box in an editorial or broadcast placement or on a package offer).	Posters and signs should not be used when message is too complex, or requires a lot of detail. Situations in which what the brochure has to say is not really useful.
SCHOOL PROMOTIONS —Teachers and students can be an important audience when the message is educational. Typical kinds of activities include study guides, posters or brochures, contests which will benefit the learning process.	Promotion of a program, event or idea which has educational value.	Situations in which youth is not an important target audience, or if message is too commercial and has no educational purpose.

Public Relations and Promotional Ideas

Public Relations Activity	Appropriate for	Not Appropriate for
PROCLAMATION OR OFFICIAL MESSAGE—A Presidential, Mayoral, or other governmental message or proclamation is used to give special designation to an idea which affects the public. Example: "Country Music Month," "National Heart Week," "Black History Month," etc.	Giving special recognition to an idea or event.	Promoting a product, or commercial message. Promoting an idea which is only of interest to a select or small group of people.
PROMOTIONAL GIMMICK—a gift or gimmick which is provided to the media or consumers, in addition to the story.	A situation in which the gimmick is intended to amuse or attract attention, or remind the recipient of a story or event.	A story of a serious nature.

Source: Sheryl Johnston Communications, Ltd.

Part V

Targeting and Selling through Direct Marketing

Specialized catalogs...home-shopping shows...interactive television...data bases that focus on the best prospects for every conceivable product and service. These are just a few of the reasons why direct marketing is the fastest-growing field in advertising. Today, every medium is benefiting from direct marketing as advertisers seek new ways to target their prime customers and communicate with them more effectively and efficiently. The 6 checklists and charts in Part V will help you determine whether direct marketing is right for your business—and how you can reap its many benefits.

32

When to Use Direct Marketing

The 1980s have seen an explosion in direct marketing which is growing faster than general advertising. It is attracting many marketers who had never previously considered using it as part of their advertising mix. Is direct marketing right for you? Ask yourself the following 19 questions. If you answer "Yes" to any one of them, indicate below the question where and how you could put it to work for you.

Is This Important to You?

	YES	NO

1. When the product or service requires a full explanation and you must communicate a message that is too complex or detailed to be conveyed in general advertising. ☐ ☐

_____

_____

2. When it is a unique product or service for which other distribution channels are either not available, too expensive or otherwise unsatisfactory. ☐ ☐

_____

_____

3. When you must produce an immediate *and* identifiable order or inquiry. ☐ ☐

_____

_____

4. When a specific, selected market of prime prospects is both definable and recognizable and where lists or media vehicles are available to target them. ☐ ☐

_____

_____

5. When a specific, selected market or target audience is desired and other media can deliver it only with excessive waste circulation. ☐ ☐

_____

_____

When to Use Direct Marketing

6. When a personal, personalized or confidential communication is desired.   ☐   ☐

_____

_____

7. When the marketing strategy calls for a format that cannot be carried in a general media buy.   ☐   ☐

_____

_____

8. When a specific market needs to be covered with a minimum of spill-over into adjacent areas.   ☐   ☐

_____

_____

9. When sampling is practical and highly desirable.   ☐   ☐

_____

_____

10. When precise timing or frequency of contact is needed.   ☐   ☐

_____

_____

11. When it is desirable to conduct research to measure effectiveness within certain markets; determine prospect profiles; or test price, packaging or potential users within a market.   ☐   ☐

_____

_____

12. When a highly controlled distribution is required.   ☐   ☐

_____

_____

When to Use Direct Marketing

	YES	NO
13. When the sale of the product directly to the prospect, without dealers or retailers, is desired.	☐	☐
14. When you want to secure leads which will be followed up by personal sales contacts or further direct mail.	☐	☐
15. When you want to direct a specific prospect to a specific location.	☐	☐
16. When you want to introduce your product or service to potential prospects in a highly personal manner.	☐	☐
17. When you want to build and refine mailing lists.	☐	☐
18. When you want to follow up inquiries secured through other media vehicles including responses to sales promotion offers.	☐	☐
19. When you want to turn the "short-term" response to a sales promotion offer into a "long-term" customer relationship and capitalize on the lifetime potential value of that customer.	☐	☐

33

Bob Stone's Tips for Direct Marketing Success (Abridged)

The success of a direct marketing effort is spelled P-L-A-N-N-I-N-G! It depends upon a myriad of factors, including the product or service, the media, the offer, the communications format, the preliminary testing, and a thorough analysis of the results. In his book *Successful Direct Marketing Methods*, Bob Stone zeros in on what makes a direct marketing effort successful. Focus on each of these tips as you plan and implement your direct marketing effort. If your efforts need improvement, use the available space to suggest new action.

The Product or Service

	YES	NO
1. Is it a real value for the price asked?	☐	☐
2. Does it stack up well against competition?	☐	☐
3. Does it have exclusive features?	☐	☐
4. Is its cost low enough to warrant a mail order markup?	☐	☐
5. Does the product or service lend itself to repeat business?	☐	☐

Bob Stone's Tips for Direct Marketing Success

The Media

	YES	NO

1. Is your customer list cleaned on a regular basis? ☐ ☐

_____

_____

2. Have you developed a profile of your customers, giving you all their important demographic characteristics? ☐ ☐

_____

_____

3. Have you coded your customer list by recency of purchase? ☐ ☐

_____

_____

4. Have you worked with competent list compilers in selecting names of prospects who match the profile of those on your customer list? ☐ ☐

_____

_____

5. Have you determined how often you can successfully mail to the same list? ☐ ☐

_____

_____

6. Have you matched your offers with your markets and selected media vehicles with good direct response track records or the potential to become good direct response vehicles? ☐ ☐

_____

_____

Bob Stone's Tips for Direct Marketing Success

	YES	NO

7. Have you continually monitored the true response of the media, computing for each vehicle the number of inquiries less returns, the net cash receipts and repeat business?　　　　☐　☐

_____

_____

8. Have you determined the best times and the best frequency for using each media vehicle?　　　　☐　☐

_____

_____

The Offers

1. Are you using the most enticing offers you can within the realm of good business?　　　　☐　☐

_____

_____

2. Does your offer lend itself to the development of an automatic repeat business cycle?　　　　☐　☐

_____

_____

3. Have you determined the ideal introductory period or quantity for your plan?　　　　☐　☐

_____

_____

4. Have you determined the ideal introductory price for your offer?　　　　☐　☐

_____

_____

Bob Stone's Tips for Direct Marketing Success

The Communication Format

	YES	NO
1. Are your mailings, ads or commercials in character with your product or service and your target market?	☐	☐
2. Does your advertising and mailing package grab attention and impel action?	☐	☐

Testing

	YES	NO
1. Do you consistently test the best product, media, offers and formats?	☐	☐
2. Have you tested the best timing and frequency of your offers?	☐	☐
3. Do you consistently test new potential consumer markets?	☐	☐
4. Have you determined the most responsive geographic areas?	☐	☐

Bob Stone's Tips for Direct Marketing Success

Analyzing the Results

	YES	NO
1. Do you track results by source?	☐	☐

_____

_____

| 2. Do you analyze results by ZIP codes and by demographics? | ☐ | ☐ |

_____

_____

| 3. Do you compute the level of repeat business by original source? | ☐ | ☐ |

_____

_____

Source: *Successful Direct Marketing Methods,* 4th edition, by Bob Stone (1988)

34

A Final Checkup for Effective Catalog Copy

A leader in catalog marketing, Maxwell Sroge has targeted 8 questions marketers should ask about their copy before a catalog goes to print. Use this checklist to test your own copy, whether it is for a catalog or for general advertising. If you answer "No" to any question, analyze the problem and remedy it. It will save you time, money and problems later on.

	YES	NO
1. Is your copy in the right, the best and the most logical order?	☐	☐

Suggested Change? _____

_____

_____

| 2. Is the copy persuasive? | ☐ | ☐ |

Suggested Change? _____

_____

_____

| 3. Is the copy complete? | ☐ | ☐ |

Suggested Change? _____

_____

_____

| 4. Is the copy clear? | ☐ | ☐ |

Suggested Change? _____

_____

_____

Checkup for Effective Catalog Copy

5. Is the copy consistent?   ☐   ☐

   Suggested Change? _____ _____

   _____

   _____

6. Is the copy accurate?   ☐   ☐

   Suggested Change? _____

   _____

   _____

7. Is the copy interesting?   ☐   ☐

   Suggested Change? _____

   _____

   _____

8. Is the copy believable?   ☐   ☐

   Suggested Change? _____

   _____

   _____

Source: *How to Create Successful Catalogs,* by Maxwell Sroge (1985)

Art or Photography in Catalogs: Which Way Should You Go?

In his book *How to Create Successful Catalogs*, Maxwell Sroge offers this advice on the advantages of art and photography in catalog illustrations. His comments are sound whenever you must choose between art and photography in a catalog or print ad.

	Which Works Best?		
	Art	Photography	Combination
1. Emphasis on product function for greater customer understanding	X		
2. Easier emphasis on product detail	X		
3. Easy addition of seasonal aspects when preparing catalogs in off seasons	X		
4. Easy illustration of benefits such as bearing fruit trees	X		
5. Greater believability with the picture of the actual product		X	
6. Heightened credibility because of seeing the real thing		X	
7. Greater customer association with the product		X	
8. Emphasis on product detail with art coupled with the realism of photography			X
9. Emphasis on function			X

Source: *How to Create Successful Catalogs*, by Maxwell Sroge (1985)

"Golden Rules" for 800-Number Success

If your direct marketing effort calls for the use of an 800 number, be sure to follow these 5 *"Golden Rules" for 800-Number Success.* They will save you time, help you avoid aggravation and pay off at your cash register.

1. Make certain the number has "rhythm" so it is easy to remember. For example, 1-800-288-8000 is far easier to remember than 1-800-647-2519 (and 1-800-CALLNOW is even better!).

2. Make certain the number is a highly visible part of the ad. If it is a commercial, make certain the number is displayed enough different times and for a long enough time to be remembered.

3. Make certain there are adequate facilities to handle incoming calls.

4. Make certain that you explain when phone calls are taken if it isn't 24 hours a day, 7 days a week.

5. Use a variety of 800 numbers for tracing the source of your calls.

12 Keys to the Effective Use of Direct Marketing Order Forms

The last step your potential customer may take in responding to a direct marketing offer is to fill out the order form. If the form is incomplete or difficult to follow, your prospect may simply say "Forget it. . .I don't really want to buy this anyway!" *12 Keys to the Effective Use of Direct Marketing Order Forms* will help you keep potential prospects from becoming lost prospects.

	YES	NO

1. Keep the order form simple and neat. ☐ ☐

   Suggested Improvement: _____

   _____

2. Make certain the spaces are large enough for the customer to fill in all the necessary information. ☐ ☐

   Suggested Improvement: _____

   _____

3. Attract readers to the order form and make it easy for them to find it. ☐ ☐

   Suggested Improvement: _____

   _____

4. Encourage your customers to print carefully. ☐ ☐

   Suggested Improvement: _____

   _____

5. Remind them to use the mailing label if you have provided one. ☐ ☐

   Suggested Improvement: _____

   _____

6. Be sure to tell the customers how to pay for their orders, how much to pay including taxes and shipping, *and* where to send the order. ☐ ☐

   Suggested Improvement: _____

   _____

The Effective Use of Direct Marketing Order Forms

7. If you are offering an exchange or a satisfaction guarantee, explain exactly what it covers and how to take advantage of it. ☐ ☐

   Suggested Improvement: _____

   _____

8. Let your customers build your list by asking them for the names of friends who might be good prospects. ☐ ☐

   Suggested Improvement: _____

   _____

9. Tell your customers how long it will take for their order to be delivered. ☐ ☐

   Suggested Improvement: _____

   _____

10. Make sure your customer knows how long the offer is good. ☐ ☐

    Suggested Improvement: _____

    _____

11. NEVER print the order form white on black since your customer's writing will not show up on it! ☐ ☐

    Suggested Improvement: _____

    _____

12. If you use an 800 number, be sure to refer to five *"Golden Rules" for 800-Number Success.* ☐ ☐

    Suggested Improvement: _____

    _____

Part VI

Maximizing the Sales Promotion Payoff

A circulation-building promotion for the *Chicago Tribune* announces "$129 Worth of Money-Saving Coupons in Next Sunday's *Tribune*!" Coupons, contests, premiums, refunds, and samples are but a few of the techniques being used today as more dollars are shifted from image and brand-building advertising to action-oriented, short-term sales promotion. To best use sales promotion, you must determine exactly what it can and can't do for your business, decide which techniques can best accomplish your goals, and measure your results. The 6 checklists and charts in Part VI will guide you through these steps and help you profitably organize your sales promotion planning process.

An 8-Step
Problem-Solving Process

In their book, *Sales Promotion Management*, Don Schultz and Bill Robinson provide an excellent process for solving sales promotion problems. This technique actually extends well beyond sales promotion, and can help solve almost any advertising problem.

1. Identify the problem.

2. Isolate the cause of the problem.

3. Set the objectives you want to accomplish in solving the problem.

4. Identify the potential solutions to the problem.

5. Evaluate the alternative solutions.

6. Develop a system of budget and control and a system for monitoring the problem-solving process.

7. Implement the program to solve the problem.

8. Measure the results.

Source: *Sales Promotion Management*, by Don E. Schultz and William A. Robinson (1982)

The Do's and Cannot Do's of Consumer Sales Promotion

During the 1980's, advertisers extensively increased their investments in sales promotion programs, both in absolute terms and often at the expense of long-term brand-building advertising. While consumer sales promotion can accomplish many objectives, there is much it cannot do. Refer to *The Do's and Cannot Do's of Consumer Sales Promotion* in determining what promotion can or cannot do for you.

Is This Important to You?

Consumer Sales Promotion *CAN*

	YES	NO
1. Reach new users.	☐	☐
2. Obtain trial for a product.	☐	☐
3. Hold onto current users of a product.	☐	☐
4. Encourage repeat usage of a product.	☐	☐
5. Build more frequent or multiple purchases of a product.	☐	☐
6. Encourage users to stock up with a big supply of a product.	☐	☐
7. Introduce a new or improved product.	☐	☐
8. Introduce new packaging or a different size package.	☐	☐
9. Neutralize competitive advertising or sales promotion.	☐	☐
10. Capitalize on seasonal, geographic or special events.	☐	☐
11. Encourage consumers to trade up to a larger size, a more profitable line, or another product in the line.	☐	☐
12. Reinforce a brand's advertising by encouraging purchase *now*!	☐	☐

Consumer Sales Promotion

Consumer Sales Promotion *CANNOT*

	YES	NO
1. Build brand loyalty or develop a long-term consumer franchise by itself.	☐	☐
2. Reverse a declining sales trend.	☐	☐
3. Change basic consumer nonacceptance of a product.	☐	☐
4. Compensate for inadequate levels of consumer advertising.	☐	☐
5. Overcome product problems in pricing, packaging, quality or performance.	☐	☐

Source: *Sales Promotion Management*, by Don E. Schultz and William A. Robinson (1982)

40

41 Consumer Sales Promotion Idea Starters

Once you decide that a consumer sales promotion program will help carry out your marketing objectives, the question becomes..."What should I do?" In developing a strategy, consider *all* options. Use this idea starter checklist by first noting techniques being used by your competitors, and then checking off programs you might consider using.

	Used by Competition	A Program We Might Use
1. Contests	☐	☐
2. Games	☐	☐
3. Instant (ruboff) sweepstakes	☐	☐
4. General sweepstakes	☐	☐
5. Prepicked winner sweepstakes	☐	☐
6. In-pack premiums	☐	☐
7. On-pack premiums	☐	☐
8. Near-pack premiums	☐	☐
9. Mail-in premiums	☐	☐
10. Self-liquidating premiums	☐	☐
11. Reusable containers	☐	☐
12. Refund on product purchase	☐	☐
13. Refund on multiple product purchase from one company	☐	☐

Consumer Sales Promotion Idea Starters

	Used by Competition	A Program We Might Use
14. Refund on related product purchase	☐	☐
15. Direct mail samples	☐	☐
16. Door-to-door samples	☐	☐
17. On-pack samples	☐	☐
18. Near-pack samples	☐	☐
19. Sample with other product purchase	☐	☐
20. Sample mail-in coupon	☐	☐
21. In-pack coupon	☐	☐
22. On-pack coupon	☐	☐
23. In-store coupon display	☐	☐
24. Cash register tape coupon	☐	☐
25. Printed shopping bag coupon	☐	☐
26. Free-standing insert coupon (FSI)	☐	☐
27. Newspaper coupon	☐	☐
28. Sunday supplement coupon	☐	☐
29. Magazine coupon	☐	☐
30. Direct mail coupon	☐	☐

Consumer Sales Promotion Idea Starters

	Used by Competition	A Program We Might Use
31. Larger size "bonus" package	☐	☐
32. Bonus unit package	☐	☐
33. Price-off label	☐	☐
34. Banded price-off pack	☐	☐
35. Trial package	☐	☐
36. Trial membership	☐	☐
37. "Buy 1 . . . Get 1 Free"	☐	☐
38. National trading stamps (S&H)	☐	☐
39. Company's own continuity plan	☐	☐
40. Store register receipt prize plan	☐	☐
41. Frequent buyer bonus plan	☐	☐

The Do's and Cannot Do's of Trade Sales Promotion

Just as consumer sales promotion grew extensively during the 1980's, trade promotion efforts have also sharply increased. Like consumer sales promotion, promotion to the trade can accomplish many objectives ...but there is much it cannot do. Refer to *The Do's and Cannot Do's of Trade Sales Promotion* in determining what it can or cannot do for you.

Is This Important to You?

TRADE SALES PROMOTION *CAN*

	YES	NO
1. Obtain feature pricing, displays and other dealer in-store support for a consumer sales promotion effort.	☐	☐
2. Help increase or reduce trade inventories.	☐	☐
3. Help obtain, expand or improve product distribution.	☐	☐
4. Motivate the sales force, dealers, brokers or wholesalers.	☐	☐
5. Improve overall trade relations	☐	☐

TRADE SALES PROMOTION *CANNOT*

	YES	NO
1. Compensate for a poorly trained sales force.	☐	☐
2. Overcome poor product distribution.	☐	☐
3. Compensate for lack of consumer advertising.	☐	☐

Source: *Sales Promotion Management*, by Don E. Schultz and William A. Robinson (1982)

42

Promotion Planning Checklist

To succeed, a well-thought-out and properly implemented promotion must cover 9 essential bases. Refer regularly to the *Promotion Planning Checklist* developed by two sales promotion pros, Bud Frankel, president of Frankel & Co., and Bill Robinson, president of William A. Robinson, Inc. With modifications, you can apply this checklist to many other marketing and communications situations.

Is This Base Covered?

	YES	NO
1. **Market Situation**	☐	☐

What is happening in the marketplace?

_____

_____

What are you doing now?

_____

_____

What is your competition doing now?

_____

_____

	YES	NO
2. **Problem to Be Solved**	☐	☐

What is the problem?

_____

_____

What is the source of the problem?

_____

_____

Promotion Planning Checklist

3. **Sales Promotion Objectives: Measurable and Unmeasurable**   ☐   ☐

Who is the consumer target? Trade target?

_____

_____

What are you trying to motivate the target to do?

_____

_____

What markets are you talking about geographically? Demographically?

_____

_____

4. **Sales Promotion Strategies**   ☐   ☐

Do they meet the objectives?

_____

_____

5. **Sales Promotion Tactics**   ☐   ☐

Do they support the strategies?

_____

_____

Do they work?

_____

_____

Are they practical?

_____

_____

Promotion Planning Checklist

Are they measurable?

_____

_____

Are they affordable?

_____

_____

6. **Timetable**   ☐   ☐

What is the sell-in deadline?

_____

_____

How long will the promotion run?

_____

_____

What is the evaluation deadline?

_____

_____

7. **Budget**   ☐   ☐

What is the anticipated budget?

_____

_____

Is there a firmly set limit?

_____

_____

Promotion Planning Checklist

Are there any unanticipated costs that could affect the budget?

_____

_____

What is the timing of requirements for funding?

_____

_____

8. **Testing**   ☐   ☐

How will the promotion be evaluated? Through pre-testing, market test or consumer groups?

_____

_____

What audience do you want to test with?

_____

_____

What are you looking for?

_____

_____

How will you evaluate whether to go with the promotion or not?

_____

_____

9. **Post-Evaluation**   ☐   ☐

How do you measure success?

_____

_____

Promotion Planning Checklist

Was there an increase in volume? Share?

_____

_____

What was the consumer response? The trade response?

_____

_____

How was the participation?

_____

_____

Source: "Promote," a feature of *Adweek's* "Marketing Week," April 13, 1987

43

13 "Never-to-Be-Forgotten" Rules for Contests and Sweepstakes

Whether you are conducting a large national sweepstakes or a small local contest, its success (and often the reputation and financial well-being of your company) can depend upon how clearly the rules are spelled out. Without this, the value of the promotion can be lost amid confusion about the entry requirements, how winners are determined and how prizes are awarded. Make certain you follow every one of the *13 "Never-to-Be-Forgotten" Rules for Contests and Sweepstakes* in running your promotion.

Is This Covered?

REQUIREMENTS TO ENTER

	YES	NO
1. Eligibility? (State "Void Where Prohibited by Law")	☐	☐
2. Material to submit? (State "All Entries Become the Property of _____")	☐	☐
3. Purchase requirements?	☐	☐
4. Number of entries?	☐	☐
5. Closing date of event?	☐	☐

DETERMINATION OF THE WINNERS

	YES	NO
1. Judging method?	☐	☐
2. Breaking of ties?	☐	☐
3. Judging organization? (State "All Decisions Are Final")	☐	☐

Rules for Contests and Sweepstakes

AWARDING OF PRIZES

	YES	NO
1. The prize structure?	☐	☐
2. Notification of winners—when and how?	☐	☐
3. Awarding of prizes—when and how?	☐	☐
4. Providing winners' names to all interested?	☐	☐
5. Provision for unclaimed prizes?	☐	☐

Source: *Sales Promotion Management*, by Don E. Schultz and William A. Robinson (1982)

Researching Your Advertising's Health and Well-Being

Advertising is aimed at generating a response from a business's customers. Sometimes the response can be measured by the ring of the cash register or the number of inquiries received. In most cases, however, the response is in terms of an intermediate measure of effectiveness such as a change in awareness or attitude toward a product or service. The 6 checklists and charts in Part VII will help you define the response you seek from your advertising; evaluate research reports and research companies; develop a simple yet practical original research project; and determine how much frequency is needed under varying creative, media and marketing conditions.

The 14-Point
Advertising Response Monitor

All advertising messages seek to elicit some form of human response from the consumer. This holds true whether the advertiser sells a product, a service or an idea, and whether the consumer is a young housewife shopping for groceries or a company executive investigating new corporate benefit plans for his firm. Use *The 14-Point Advertising Response Monitor* to evaluate the performance of your advertising. In the columns to the right, indicate how well you feel your advertising is communicating. Then note in the space below how you might improve its performance.

Was the Advertising Received?

	Yes	Maybe	No
1. Did it catch the consumer's eye? His or her ear?	☐	☐	☐

_____

_____

| 2. Did it catch his or her attention? | ☐ | ☐ | ☐ |

_____

_____

| 3. Did it get through? | ☐ | ☐ | ☐ |

_____

_____

| 4. Was it remembered? | ☐ | ☐ | ☐ |

_____

_____

Was the Advertising Comprehended?

| 5. Was it understood? | ☐ | ☐ | ☐ |

_____

_____

The Advertising Response Monitor

	Yes	Maybe	No
6. Did the consumer "get the message"?	☐	☐	☐

_____

_____

| 7. Was the message identified with the product, the service or the idea? | ☐ | ☐ | ☐ |

_____

_____

| 8. Was anything confusing or unclear? | ☐ | ☐ | ☐ |

_____

_____

Did the Advertising Make an Impression?

| 9. Did the consumer accept the proposition? | ☐ | ☐ | ☐ |

_____

_____

| 10. Did the advertising affect attitudes toward the product, the service or the idea? | ☐ | ☐ | ☐ |

_____

_____

| 11. Did the consumer think or feel differently about the product, the service or the idea after exposure? | ☐ | ☐ | ☐ |

_____

_____

The Advertising Response Monitor

	Yes	Maybe	No
12. Did the advertising affect perceptions of the product, the service or the idea?	☐	☐	☐
13. Did the advertising alter perceptions of the competing products, services or ideas?	☐	☐	☐
14. Did the consumer respond to direct action appeals?	☐	☐	☐

_____

_____

Source: The PACT (Positioning Advertising Copy Testing) Agencies Report (1982)

An 18-Point Checkup on the Use of Research Reports

Research is the backbone of much of the work done in advertising and public relations. While not everyone is a trained researcher, all of us should understand what constitutes good, fair and unbiased research. Before using any research report, read the following "18-Point Checkup" to determine if it is in "good working order." First, check whether you feel each item is dealt with properly. Then, note any further information you need to determine whether or not to use the report.

	YES	NO
1. Does the report identify the organization that initiated and paid for the research?	☐	☐
2. Is there a statement of the purpose of the research that clearly states what it was meant to accomplish?	☐	☐
3. Are the organizations which designed and were responsible for conducting the research identified?	☐	☐
4. Is there a full description, in nontechnical language, of the research design, including a definition of what is measured and how the data are collected?	☐	☐
5. Is the design evenhanded; that is, is it free of leading questions and other bias; does it address questions of fact and opinion without inducing answers that unfairly benefit the study sponsors?	☐	☐

Checkup on the Use of Research Reports

	YES	NO
6. Does it address questions which respondents are capable of answering?	☐	☐

_____

_____

| 7. Does the sample represent the population it is meant to represent? | ☐ | ☐ |

_____

_____

| 8. Does the report specify the proportion of the designated sample from which information was collected and processed or say that the proportion cannot be determined? | ☐ | ☐ |

_____

_____

| 9. Were those who collected data kept free of clues to the study sponsorship or the expected responses, or other leads or information that might condition or bias the information they obtained and recorded? | ☐ | ☐ |

_____

_____

| 10. Was the sample large enough to provide stable findings? | ☐ | ☐ |

_____

_____

| 11. Are sampling error limits shown, if they can be computed? | ☐ | ☐ |

_____

_____

| 12. Does the report specify when the data were collected? | ☐ | ☐ |

_____

_____

Checkup on the Use of Research Reports

	YES	NO

13. Does the report say clearly whether its findings do or do not apply beyond the direct source of the data? ☐ ☐

_____

_____

14. If the research has limited applications, is there a statement covering who or what it represents and the times or conditions under which it applies? ☐ ☐

_____

_____

15. Are the measurements described in simple and direct language? ☐ ☐

_____

_____

16. Are the actual findings clearly differentiated from the interpretation of the findings? ☐ ☐

_____

_____

17. Have all of the relevant findings been released, including all information potentially unfavorable to the sponsor or embarrassing to the responsible researcher? ☐ ☐

_____

_____

18. Has the research been fairly presented? ☐ ☐

_____

_____

Source: *Guidelines for the Public Use of Market and Opinion Research*, by the Advertising Research Foundation (1981)

46

11 Questions to Ask When Hiring a Research Company

At some time in your career, you may be called upon to hire a research company to conduct work for you. In deciding whom to employ, you should rely both on the recommendations of others and your own judgment. Use the following 11 questions as a guide in interviewing prospective research firms, noting any additional information you need to make an intelligent business decision.

1. Does the company have the technical competence to handle the work?

   _____

   _____

2. Have they demonstrated skill, common sense and good judgment in handling other people's work and/or problems?

   _____

   _____

3. Will they seek imaginative and creative solutions to problems rather than simply relying upon techniques that have been used in the past?

   _____

   _____

4. How important will your business be to the company?

   _____

   _____

5. Who will be working on your business, and how comfortable do you feel with them?

   _____

   _____

Hiring a Research Company

6. How qualified is the company to analyze and summarize the research in clear, concise and accurate terms?

_____

_____

7. Is the company familiar enough with your business to avoid making basic, logical mistakes of judgment?

_____

_____

8. Is the company honest? Will it do the kind of work that is correct rather than what it thinks you want to receive?

_____

_____

9. Will the company avoid providing you with excess "bells and whistles" that you neither want nor need? However, will it not cut corners by failing to ask enough questions or using samples that are either too small or not representative of the market you want to survey?

_____

_____

10. Can you trust the company to keep confidential the results of any work it does for you?

_____

_____

11. Is there anything about the company that concerns you that you have not asked?

_____

_____

47

7 Fresh Ideas for a Simple, Homegrown Research Project

Marketers must continually seek out new research techniques to find fresh answers to old questions. Much can be gained by simply going out and talking to people. The following ideas will suggest non-traditional, fast and inexpensive ways of learning what your customers are thinking and doing. Be sure to note *your* ideas in the spaces provided.

		YES	NO
1.	Can any research be easily done by your own staff in your own office?	☐	☐

_____

_____

_____

2. Can you quickly go to a location during lunch, over the weekend or after work and find exactly the kinds of people to whom you want to talk? ☐ ☐

_____

_____

_____

3. Will you be attending an event at which others there represent exactly the people you would like to survey? ☐ ☐

_____

_____

_____

4. Would any of the media you deal with have enough interest in your project to help fund it? ☐ ☐

_____

_____

_____

Ideas for a Homegrown Research Project

5. Is there a college or university with whom you could work on the project? ☐ ☐

_____

_____

_____

6. Will you be attending a conference or convention where you could slip a questionnaire under the attendees' room doors? ☐ ☐

_____

_____

_____

7. Do you and your associates personally know key people who would answer your questions if you just asked them? ☐ ☐

_____

_____

_____

The Retailer's Advertising Impact Scorecard

A small local retailer may try many different forms of advertising, but may not be sure what drew the most customers into his store. *The Retailer's Advertising Impact Scorecard* is a do-it-yourself survey that can help you track where your business comes from. When a customer calls or comes into the store, just ask "Would you tell me how you learned about our sale (or this new merchandise)?" or "Where have you heard about us lately?" Then check off each response on your *Scorecard*.

Check as Many Sources of Information as Appropriate

Newspapers	☐	☐	☐	☐	☐	☐	☐	☐	☐	☐	☐	☐	☐	☐	☐
Magazines	☐	☐	☐	☐	☐	☐	☐	☐	☐	☐	☐	☐	☐	☐	☐
Radio	☐	☐	☐	☐	☐	☐	☐	☐	☐	☐	☐	☐	☐	☐	☐
TV	☐	☐	☐	☐	☐	☐	☐	☐	☐	☐	☐	☐	☐	☐	☐
Cable	☐	☐	☐	☐	☐	☐	☐	☐	☐	☐	☐	☐	☐	☐	☐
Direct Mail	☐	☐	☐	☐	☐	☐	☐	☐	☐	☐	☐	☐	☐	☐	☐
Yellow Pages	☐	☐	☐	☐	☐	☐	☐	☐	☐	☐	☐	☐	☐	☐	☐
Outdoor Boards	☐	☐	☐	☐	☐	☐	☐	☐	☐	☐	☐	☐	☐	☐	☐
Word-of-Mouth	☐	☐	☐	☐	☐	☐	☐	☐	☐	☐	☐	☐	☐	☐	☐
_____	☐	☐	☐	☐	☐	☐	☐	☐	☐	☐	☐	☐	☐	☐	☐
_____	☐	☐	☐	☐	☐	☐	☐	☐	☐	☐	☐	☐	☐	☐	☐
_____	☐	☐	☐	☐	☐	☐	☐	☐	☐	☐	☐	☐	☐	☐	☐
_____	☐	☐	☐	☐	☐	☐	☐	☐	☐	☐	☐	☐	☐	☐	☐
_____	☐	☐	☐	☐	☐	☐	☐	☐	☐	☐	☐	☐	☐	☐	☐
_____	☐	☐	☐	☐	☐	☐	☐	☐	☐	☐	☐	☐	☐	☐	☐

How Much Frequency Is Enough?

"How much frequency is enough?" While there is no one answer to this question, with too little repetition an ad may have little impact on the consumer. With excessive repetition, an ad can lose its ability to effectively communicate, persuade or create positive attitudes.

The following checklist can guide you in determining frequency. Examine the 21 message, media and market-related factors and check the boxes that apply to you. Then analyze your competition in the same manner. (The overall scoring of attributes is highly subjective.) The goal is to see the degree to which the "more" factors outweigh the "less" factors in your specific case. . .*and* to determine whether you may need more or less frequency than your competition.

When You Need MORE Frequency			When You Need LESS Frequency
Message Factors			
New advertising campaign	☐	☐	Older advertising campaign
Many different themes	☐	☐	A single theme
Complicated message	☐	☐	Simple message
Long message	☐	☐	Short message
Small size	☐	☐	Large size
Low-keyed, nonabrasive	☐	☐	Intrusive
Similar to competition	☐	☐	Different from competition
General image advertising	☐	☐	Specific product sell
Nonemotional content	☐	☐	Highly emotional message
Media Factors			
Exposure in many media	☐	☐	Exposure in few media
Flighted schedule	☐	☐	Continuity schedule
Highly cluttered environment	☐	☐	Uncluttered environment
Noncompatible environment	☐	☐	Compatible editorial setting
Low attention-holding media	☐	☐	High attention-holding media

How Much Frequency Is Enough?

When You Need MORE Frequency			When You Need LESS Frequency
Market Factors			
Infrequently purchased product	☐	☐	Frequently purchased product
Low-interest product	☐	☐	High-interest product
New product	☐	☐	Established product
Strong competition	☐	☐	Limited competition
A minor brand in category	☐	☐	A major brand in category
Infrequently used product	☐	☐	Frequently used product
Limited promotional activity	☐	☐	High promotional activity
Overall Frequency Skew	☐	☐	

Part VIII

Communicating to Win

"It's not just what you know...it's how you show you know it!"

It's simple, but true: in advertising, communication is critical. To succeed, you must write well, present well, negotiate well, *and* build lasting relationships with your clients and customers. The 12 checklists and charts in Part VIII will help you polish all aspects of your communications skills.

50

14 Tips to a Winning Presentation

Whether you are speaking before hundreds in a hotel ballroom or a single client in a conference room, the success of your presentation depends on more than what you have to say. How you say it and how you interact with your audience also determine their response. These 14 guidelines are aimed at making you and your presentation winners with your audience.

1. Be sure to tell your audience why your presentation is relevant to them.

2. Keep your presentation within or under the amount of time you have been allowed. Research indicates that adult concentration peaks out at 1 hour and 15 minutes. If you plan to allow 30 minutes for questions and discussion, spend no more than 45 minutes on your formal presentation.

3. Do not tell jokes unless you are a great storyteller...and then make certain that your story will offend absolutely no one in the room!

4. Remember that most audiences do not settle down right away. Don't make clever statements and important points in the first minutes of your presentation.

5. Eliminate all material that is not directly relevant to the central theme of your presentation.

6. Your visual aids should be aids and not crutches. Do not overwhelm your audience with them.

7. Make certain the visual aids are large enough for everyone in the audience to see and simple enough for everyone to understand.

8. Visuals should relate only to that portion of the presentation you are covering at a particular point in time. Never permit your audience to look ahead on the screen to something you are not yet ready to discuss.

9. Maintain eye contact with your audience throughout your presentation.

10. Make sure your podium microphone and light are in good working order.

11. During the question period, you are bound to hear from people who aren't really asking questions, but are giving a speech designed to show how much they know or how much more they know than do you. Respect them, but never be defensive. Emphasize the points upon which you agree and point out those which you do not agree with.

12. Listen actively to audience questions. Often, the questioner is asking more than what meets the ear.

13. Always rephrase what you think the question to be before you respond to it.

14. Expect to have pictures taken at many events where you will speak. Dress professionally and in colors that photograph well. This means dark colors rather than light tones, contrasting shirts and blouses, and bright ties or scarves.

Guidelines for Using Numbers in Presentations

In more than one presentation, you've probably seen a number and wondered where it came from, what it meant, and what you were expected to do with it. Follow these guidelines and you will have won the battle of figure frustration!

1. Make certain to indicate where the numbers come from.

2. When you are showing a trend, define its base period exactly.

3. When you show percentages or index numbers, be sure to include the real numbers themselves to avoid any misleading assumptions.

4. Be sure to show long-term trends and not just averages at one or two points in time.

5. Use the most up-to-date numbers you have, but if they are not typical of a long-term trend, be sure to indicate so.

6. Since most people have trouble with numbers, use tables, charts, and graphs whenever possible.

7. When you use tables, use several of them rather than crowding everything into one.

8. Bring the numbers alive and clearly explain to everyone what they mean.

52

The "Never-to-Be-Forgotten" Pocket Presentation Planner

As the name implies, this should be carried into every meeting where an upcoming presentation may be discussed. Its purpose is to make certain that when you leave the meeting, you can pass on to your associates just what the presentation will cover and what is expected of whom.

THE OCCASION

Purpose of the Presentation?

_____

_____

_____

When?

_____

_____

_____

Where?

_____

_____

_____

How Long?

_____

_____

_____

The Pocket Presentation Planner

THE AUDIENCE

Who?

_____

_____

_____

How Many?

_____

_____

_____

Knowledge of Subject?

_____

_____

_____

Background?

_____

_____

_____

Going-In Opinions?

_____

_____

_____

The Pocket Presentation Planner

WHAT TO INCLUDE

Information?	Provided by Whom?	Ways to Visualize?

53

9 Tips on Negotiating to Win

In a negotiation, there is one basic objective. . . to win. And the key to winning is having a leg up in terms of knowledge and technique. While volumes have been written on how to negotiate, success in the end really depends on these two points. By carefully considering each of the following questions, you'll get that leg up and prepare yourself for even the toughest negotiation.

	YES	NO
1. Are you absolutely sure you are negotiating with the right person—the person with the power?	☐	☐
2. Do you have any insights into the people you are negotiating with that can help you win?	☐	☐
3. Do you know what you really want to accomplish?	☐	☐
4. Do you know what you are really willing to give in on to accomplish this?	☐	☐
5. Have you done all of your homework and gathered all of the facts you need to support your position?	☐	☐

		YES	NO
6.	Are you negotiating on neutral turf?	☐	☐

_____

_____

7.	Is time on your side or are you being pressured to make a fast decision?	☐	☐

_____

_____

8.	Will you be able to convince the other side that if you win, they won't lose—or better still, that if you win, they win?	☐	☐

_____

_____

9.	Are you certain that now is the best time to be entering into the negotiation?	☐	☐

_____

_____

54

11 Guidelines for Winning at New Business

An advertising agency's growth depends on how well it keeps its existing clients satisfied and how successfully it wins new business. Often, the difference between winning and losing a new business presentation is small— so small that the losing agency may say, "If only I had . . . ." These *11 Guidelines for Winning at New Business* will improve your odds.

1. Focus exclusively on the client, his or her concerns and interests throughout the presentation. The client doesn't really care how wonderful you are. What the client does care about is what's in it for him or her.

   Notes:

2. Every good salesperson knows that if you don't get your customer's attention right at the start, you may have lost him or her forever. Each minute counts so don't waste a precious second by being boring or irrelevant.

   Notes:

3. Never let your audiovisuals dominate the presentation. In the end, it is the person-to-person chemistry that is critical.

   Notes:

4. Don't overdo the case histories. If a case study cannot be related to the client's business and how you can help make it grow, don't use up time presenting it.

   Notes:

5. Avoid showing too much of your work. Every agency you compete with can be expected to show its very best work—so thin out anything that isn't your very, very best.

   Notes:

6. Don't line up too many presenters. It is difficult to tell someone who has worked hard pulling a presentation together that he or she won't be in the meeting itself. But clients do not like to feel overwhelmed. Limit your team to a small number of professionals who are first-rate presenters and who will play a significant role in the meeting.

   Notes:

7. If the meeting is on your turf, make sure the physical surroundings are comfortable. If the first thing a prospective client says is, "It's too hot in here," you face an uphill battle.

   Notes:

8. Every agency will promise A+ work. Just as one brand must differentiate itself from others in its category, your agency must offer a unique focus that separates it from the competition.

   Notes:

9. Sell the steak, but don't forget that the sizzle may get you the business. Given the choice between a dull, dependable shop and an exciting, slightly risky agency, excitement will usually win out.

   Notes:

10. At one time, large, full-service agencies regarded other large, full-service agencies as their only competition. No longer. Today, advertisers can provide many of the services offered by the larger agencies in-house or through independent media services and consultants. Don't overdue bigness!

    Notes:

11. And finally, never *ever* forget to let your prospective client know that you really want their business. And never forget to ask for the order!

    Notes:

<table>
<tr><td></td><td></td></tr>
</table>

55

29 Ways for an Agency to Establish Good Client Relations

Mergers, acquisitions, increasing profit pressure and advertiser unrest have made the need for strong agency-client relations greater than ever. During her first three years in account management at DDB Needham Worldwide, Roberta Kaatz compiled this list of *29 Ways for an Agency to Establish Good Client Relations.* Use it to check up on the state of your agency–client marriage. Note the rocky areas, and focus on how you can build a stronger relationship in the future. Much of this is just pure common sense. But unfortunately, common sense is what we too often overlook in our relations with one another!

Should I Work on This?

	YES	NO
1. Be dependable.	☐	☐
2. Be knowledgeable about your agency's resources.	☐	☐
3. Be knowledgeable about your client's business.	☐	☐
4. Cultivate a team spirit between you and your immediate counterpart at the client.	☐	☐
5. Be honest. Never lie to your client.	☐	☐
6. Be proactive and show initiative. Don't just take orders from your client.	☐	☐
7. Be a problem solver, not a problem maker!	☐	☐
8. Be perceptive. Know your client's likes, dislikes, and idiosyncrasies.	☐	☐
9. Champion the development of outstanding work for your client by your agency.	☐	☐
10. Be friends with your client.	☐	☐
11. Go that extra mile beyond simply fulfilling your client's requests.	☐	☐
12. Make your client look good in front of his boss and his management.	☐	☐
13. Know your client's birthday, anniversary and favorite restaurants.	☐	☐
14. Be human and be yourself, so that the client does not see you as a clone of the agency.	☐	☐

140

Ways to Establish Good Client Relations

	YES	NO
15. Keep your client up-to-date and knowledgeable about what's happening in advertising. Send him or her articles, commercials, examples of great and bad advertising.	☐	☐
16. Make sure your client believes you are truly an advertising expert.	☐	☐
17. Do the little things that make a difference, like bringing in the donuts for an early morning meeting.	☐	☐
18. Don't constantly badger your client about the need to spend more in media. Be ready to make the point when the time is right, but don't beat it into the ground.	☐	☐
19. Develop a good relationship with your client's secretary.	☐	☐
20. Return your client's phone calls within a reasonable period of time.	☐	☐
21. Know the names of all your client's children.	☐	☐
22. Explain why something can't be done in a certain way by a certain time—but don't make excuses.	☐	☐
23. Never copy your client's supervisor without telling him or her you are doing so.	☐	☐
24. Don't use old advertising cliches like "impactful," "proactive," and "we're really excited about this breakthrough creative."	☐	☐
25. Don't promise that which you know cannot be delivered.	☐	☐
26. Don't cry wolf by always getting excited about everything. Save your steam for the things that really count.	☐	☐
27. Help your client develop close relationships with all the key people at the agency who work on his or her business.	☐	☐
28. Don't be so intent on winning every battle with your client that you eventually lose the war.	☐	☐
29. Be enthusiastic!	☐	☐

When Should You Put It in Writing?

In today's business climate, there is a constant conflict between the desire to keep it simple and the tendency to overdo it. This affects the communications process when you must decide between putting a message in writing or conveying it in person or over the phone. Since time is money, your decision should depend upon your answers to the following 8 questions. If you answer "Yes" to any one of them, write it out!

	YES	NO
1. Are you concerned that what you have to say will not be understood or properly acted upon?	☐	☐
2. If the message is misunderstood, will it cost you time and/or money?	☐	☐
3. Are you asking people to spend their own time and/or money on something?	☐	☐
4. Are you attempting to change a way of doing something that has been long understood and accepted?	☐	☐
5. Do a large number of people need to receive, understand and act upon the same message?	☐	☐
6. Will you and the people who follow you need to know what was said in the days, weeks, months and years ahead?	☐	☐
7. Is what you have to say more than just a routine request or question?	☐	☐
8. Will you sleep better knowing that it is in writing?	☐	☐

57 A 3-Step Approach to More Effective Business Writing

Whether you write business reports, memos and letters every day or just once in a while, this 3-step approach can make writing easier and make what you write more effective. Just remember, *follow all 3 steps*. Prewriting is as essential as the actual writing itself—and without revising, the most important document may be hopelessly unprofessional.

Step One: Prewriting

In prewriting, you are defining your concept and gathering facts that will serve as material for step two, writing. Ask yourself these questions first.

1. What is the purpose of what you are writing? Why are you writing it?

2. Who is the audience you want to inform or influence? What are their interests and motivations? How much knowledge and interest will they have in what you say?

3. What do you want to say, and what is the scope of the project?

4. How much and what kind of background research data do you need to gather?

Step Two: Writing

Once you have established your purpose, identified your audience, defined your topic, and gathered your data, you are ready to write.

1. Determine how you can most effectively organize the material to clearly and completely communicate what you have to say.

2. Outline what you want to say in the order you want to say it.

3. Write the first draft, concentrating on developing what you want to say and not concentrating on the exact form in which you say it.

Step Three: Revising

When you begin to revise your material, keep in mind that you are reading it primarily from the *reader's* point of view.

1. Edit and check the draft several times for clarity, tone, accuracy and brevity. Have you included everything your reader will want to know to make a decision?

2. Check for grammar, spelling errors and other careless mistakes.

3. Make sure the final copy is neat and free from erasures, typos and other marks.

Source: *Handbook for Business Writing,* by L. Sue Baugh, Maridell Fryar and David Thomas (1986)

A 7-Step Approach to Writing for Information

When you write for information, you want the person receiving your letter to understand what you need and send the material out to you promptly. Follow these 7 steps to avoid needless confusion and back-and-forth communication.

1. Clearly state exactly what type of information you are requesting.

2. Ask only for that information you believe the respondent will be able to supply.

3. Explain why you need the information and why it is important for the person you are writing to supply it.

4. Express your appreciation for the time they have taken to read and consider your request.

5. Let your reader know a realistic date by which you need to receive the information.

6. Indicate your willingness to cover the cost of any materials the reader may send you.

7. When you feel it is appropriate, include a self-addressed, stamped envelope. It is thoughtful, helpful and can often speed up the delivery of the information to you.

Source: *Handbook for Business Writing*, by L. Sue Baugh, Maridell Fryar and David Thomas (1986)

59

A 4-Step Checklist for Writing an Effective Sales Letter

The growing focus on direct marketing has resulted in a dramatic increase in the number of sales letters delivered to mailboxes across the country every day of the week. An effective sales letter represents money in the cash register and this *4-Step Checklist for Writing an Effective Sales Letter* can help ring the register for you.

Step One: Grab the Reader's Attention

	YES	NO

1. Have you identified the reader's needs and interests? ☐ ☐

   Suggested Improvement: _____

   _____

   _____

2. What benefits does your product or service offer the reader? ☐ ☐

   Suggested Improvement: _____

   _____

   _____

3. Can you state the benefit in a question or arresting statement? ☐ ☐

   Suggested Improvement: _____

   _____

   _____

Step Two: Interest the Reader in What You Have to Say

1. What motivations are you addressing—profit, savings, comfort, convenience, prestige or something else? ☐ ☐

   Suggested Improvement: _____

   _____

   _____

Checklist for Writing an Effective Sales Letter

2. If the reader has a problem you have identified, does your product or service offer a solution?   ☐   ☐

   Suggested Improvement: _____

   _____

   _____

3. Did you point out what emotional satisfaction the reader would gain from your product or service?   ☐   ☐

   Suggested Improvement: _____

   _____

   _____

Step Three: Create Desire for What You Are Selling

1. Have you supported your statements with interesting facts, statistics, tests and/or testimonials?   ☐   ☐

   Suggested Improvement: _____

   _____

   _____

2. Did you offer any warranty, money-back promise or evidence of your support for your product or service?   ☐   ☐

   Suggested Improvement: _____

   _____

   _____

Checklist for Writing an Effective Sales Letter

Step Four: Ask the Reader to Take Action Now!   YES   NO

1. What specific action do you want the reader to take?   ☐   ☐

   Suggested Improvement: _____

   _____

   _____

2. Did you avoid alternative or ambiguous choices?   ☐   ☐

   Suggested Improvement: _____

   _____

   _____

3. Have you made it easy for the reader to act?   ☐   ☐

   Suggested Improvement: _____

   _____

   _____

4. Is your desired action the last sentence in the letter?   ☐   ☐

   Suggested Improvement: _____

   _____

   _____

Source: *Handbook for Business Writing,* by L. Sue Baugh, Maridell Fryar and David Thomas (1986)

7 Tips for More Productive Meetings

Advertising people constantly complain about the meetings they attend—how most of them are boring, unnecessary and too time consuming. The secret to a good meeting is having a plan and sticking to it. That's what these *7 Tips for More Productive Meetings* are all about.

1. Before calling a meeting, ask yourself, "Is this meeting really necessary?"

2. If it is, then be sure to have a written agenda. Distribute it in advance so everyone knows what will be covered.

3. Invite only those people to the meeting who need to be there.

4. If you have lots of material to cover, take care of the easiest, most positive items first.

5. Since you have an agenda, stick to it!

6. Never end a meeting without evaluating it. What was good? What was bad? What will you change at the next meeting?

7. Finally, always remember that if you call a meeting, it is your meeting to lead. Run it. Don't let it run you.

6 Tips for Efficient Filing

The most common complaints about filing systems are "I am saving too many things" and "I can't find anything I have saved!" These *6 Tips for Efficient Filing* should help alleviate both problems.

1. What information do you absolutely need to have right in your office at your fingertips?

   _____

   _____

2. What material can you keep in files outside your office?

   _____

   _____

3. What material is being kept (or should be kept) by other people?

   _____

   _____

4. What material should be thrown out?

   _____

   _____

5. Have you kept a list of your major file labels so you know what you have and where it is?

   _____

   _____

6. Is there a system to your filing that others can figure out?

   _____

   _____

Part IX

The Job, Money and Travel Survival Kit

Life in advertising is far more hectic today than it was at the beginning of the 1980's. This book would, therefore, never be complete without a *personal* survival kit. That's what Part IX is all about. It focuses exclusively on Y-O-U. Its 8 checklists and charts are aimed at getting a job, traveling on business and saving on income tax.

The Job Hunting
Action Planner

Mergers and acquisitions, consolidations and a fluctuating economy have dramatically affected employment opportunities in the advertising industry. Executive recruiters emphasize the importance of following an organized and systematic approach in the job hunt process. *The Job Hunting Action Planner* will keep your job search on track while you plan your next step. Individual sheets should be kept for each company, and the appropriate spaces should be filled out after each meeting or phone conversation.

Company _____

Address _____

Name and Title _____

_____

Department _____

Phone _____

Secretary _____

Action _____

_____

Date _____

Results _____

_____

Next Step _____

_____

Comments _____

_____

The Resume Planning Form

A resume, your "Personal Presentation in Print," should give the most complete picture possible of who you are and what you can contribute to a company. It should be concise, easy to follow, attractive and act as an enticement to your prospective employer to want to find out more about you. Experience has shown that the following one-page format works very well.

Name _____

Address _____

_____

Telephone _____ (Day)

_____ (Night)

Job Objective

_____

Experience

Job Title _____ Dates _____

Employer _____

Duties & Accomplishments _____

_____

_____

Experience

Job Title _____ Dates _____

Employer _____

Duties & Accomplishments _____

_____

_____

The Resume Planning Form

Experience

Job Title _____ Dates _____

Employer _____

Duties & Accomplishments _____

_____

_____

Education (Number as relevant)

Degree _____ Dates _____

School _____

Major _____

Minor _____

Education (Number as relevant)

Degree _____ Dates _____

School _____

Major _____

Minor _____

Special Skills and Interests

_____

Honors, Awards, Publications, Presentations

_____

Relevant Personal Information

_____

References (Optional)

_____

11 Questions to Ask Yourself about a Prospective Employee

Interviewing a prospective job candidate can be a very tough assignment. A company is often so anxious to fill a slot that it leaps to hire without looking hard enough at the kind of job a prospect can be expected to do. Ask yourself each of the following questions before making that crucial final hiring decision. If you answer "No" to any question, rethink your decision and get a second opinion. And remember: if *you* are interviewing for a job, your prospective employer will want to know *your* answers to these same questions!

	YES	NO
1. When I put together everything I know about this person, do I really believe he or she can do the job?	☐	☐

Why? _____

_____

2. Will this person quickly learn how to handle new responsibilities and respond to change?	☐	☐

Why? _____

_____

3. Does this person really want this job more than any other position?	☐	☐

Why? _____

_____

4. Does he or she want to work for our company or is it merely a stepping-stone to another company?	☐	☐

Why? _____

_____

5. Does the candidate have the education, training and experience for the job?	☐	☐

Why? _____

_____

Questions to Ask about a Prospective Employee

	YES	NO
6. Does he or she have the specific skills and knowledge needed to carry out the job effectively and efficiently? Why? _____ _____	☐	☐
7. Does the candidate lead a balanced life with interests that extend beyond work? Why? _____ _____	☐	☐
8. Will he or she get along with superiors, fellow workers, subordinates, and clients? Why? _____ _____	☐	☐
9. Will the candidate think for himself or herself, act on what he or she thinks and know when to consult with the boss? Why? _____ _____	☐	☐
10. Will this person be sensitive to the traditions of the company and to its ways of doing things? Why? _____ _____	☐	☐
11. Will the job candidate's skills and knowledge fit in with those of other employees and will he or she fill in the gaps that need filling? Why? _____ _____	☐	☐

Source: *How to Have a Winning Job Interview*, by Deborah Perlmutter Bloch (1987)

65

The Advertising Executive's Income Tax Saver

It's not what you make, it's what you keep! And there are a whole host of deductible items everyone in the advertising business should be aware of. Just remember that they must be itemized and related to your business, and that they are subject to limitations imposed by the IRS.

	This Applies to Me	
	YES	NO
Video recorder	☐	☐
Television set	☐	☐
Camera (regular and video)	☐	☐
Personal computer	☐	☐
Audio tape recorder	☐	☐
Stereo	☐	☐
Tapes	☐	☐
Video rentals and membership dues	☐	☐
Cable television costs	☐	☐
Your portfolio and reels	☐	☐
Foul weather gear for filming commercials on location	☐	☐
Theater, movie and sporting event tickets used as a part of client research	☐	☐
Membership dues	☐	☐
Award show entry fees	☐	☐
Books, professional magazines and newspapers	☐	☐
Home office furniture, desk, cabinets	☐	☐
Office pictures	☐	☐
Frames for award certificates	☐	☐
Club and credit card dues	☐	☐
Home telephone calls	☐	☐
Telephone answering machine	☐	☐

The Advertising Executive's Income Tax Saver

	YES	NO
Home entertaining	☐	☐
Tux rental and the cost of cleaning formal wear	☐	☐
Parking at office to have car available for client business	☐	☐
All free lance and research expenses, including travel, resumes and out-of-town meals	☐	☐
Business gifts and gifts to secretary (up to $25 each)	☐	☐
Nonreimbursed business expenses	☐	☐

Other items I want to ask my accountant about:

	YES	NO
_____	☐	☐
_____	☐	☐
_____	☐	☐
_____	☐	☐
_____	☐	☐
_____	☐	☐
_____	☐	☐
_____	☐	☐
_____	☐	☐
_____	☐	☐
_____	☐	☐
_____	☐	☐
_____	☐	☐

Source: *Pay Less Tax Legally*, by Barry R. Steiner, CPA

66

The Not-to-Be-Forgotten
Business Traveler's Checklist

If you've never had to buy a tube of toothpaste, a shirt or a pair of sunglasses on a business trip, you're in the minority. And if you have, you know how aggravating it is. It takes time, and you pay twice as much at your hotel as you would at home. The solution to the problem? *The Not-to-Be-Forgotten Business Traveler's Checklist.* It's guaranteed to save you time, money and frustration.

Men's Clothing	Women's Clothing	Toiletries & Accessories
Suits	Suits	Toothbrush/Toothpaste
Sports Jackets	Skirts	Deodorant
Slacks	Dresses	Shampoo
Shirts	Slacks	Conditioner
Sweaters	Blouses	Razor and Blades
Shoes	Sweaters	Shaving Cream
Socks	Shoes	Hair Dryer
Slippers	Stockings	Curlers
Pajamas	Slippers	Makeup
Robe	Nightgown	Personal Products
Underwear	Robe	Comb and Brush
Ties	Underclothing	Extra Glasses/Sun Glasses
Belts	Scarves and Ties	Tanning Lotion/Sunscreen
Sportswear	Belts	Camera and Film
Handkerchiefs	Sportswear	Travel Tickets
Jacket	Handkerchiefs	Passport
Hat	Jacket	Alarm Clock
Raincoat	Hat	Sports Equipment
Boots or Rubbers	Raincoat	Umbrella
Formal Wear	Boots or Rubbers	Work to Be Done

_____ _____ _____

_____ _____ _____

_____ _____ _____

_____ _____ _____

_____ _____ _____

_____ _____ _____

_____ _____ _____

67

Fitness on the Move

Out-of-town trips may cut into your normal exercise routine, but business travel need not result in fitness travail. A brisk, 15- to 20-minute walk can help your heart, your lungs, your blood pressure *and* your waistline. It can make you feel better, think better and perform better. Just keep the following points in mind.

1. Dress comfortably and wear sturdy running or walking shoes.

2. Stretch and bend for a few minutes to warm up before your walk.

3. Walk with your toes pointed straight ahead, head up, back straight, arms loosely swinging at your side.

4. Take long, easy strides. You're not out to break any time or distance records.

5. Breathe steadily and deeply. If you feel out of breath, *slow down*.

6. Walk before eating. Never exercise immediately after a meal.

7. Relax and have fun. Don't make your walk work!

68

The Business Traveler's Basic Health Kit

Advertising people do a lot of traveling. And one of life's great frustrations is finding yourself in a strange city in need of medication. You will probably remember to take along the obvious. But before you leave home, contact your doctor or pharmacist for specific recommendations as to what you should take with you to prevent or control less familiar problems.

	Needed?	Recommended Medication
Headaches	_____	_____
Earaches	_____	_____
Diarrhea	_____	_____
Indigestion and stomach upset	_____	_____
Ulcers	_____	_____
Skin infections	_____	_____
Eye infections	_____	_____
Vaginitis	_____	_____
Colds	_____	_____
Pain relief	_____	_____
Fever	_____	_____
Nasal congestion	_____	_____
Sinus pain	_____	_____
Motion sickness	_____	_____
Dehydration	_____	_____
Insomnia	_____	_____
Sun protection	_____	_____
Insect protection	_____	_____
Water purification	_____	_____
Tooth fillings and inlays (temporary fillings)	_____	_____
Eyeglasses (extra pair and repair kit)	_____	_____
Bandages	_____	_____
Sanitary products	_____	_____
Condoms	_____	_____

12 Tips to Keep Long-Distance Travel from Becoming Travail

Always remember that only two letters separate "travel" from "travail," so R-E-L-A-X and follow these 12 tips for a far more productive and enjoyable business trip.

1. Plan ahead. When flying across several time zones, adjust your bedtime a few days before your flight. Turn in earlier if going west—later if heading east.

2. Even before arriving at your destination, begin thinking on its time schedule in terms of what you do, drink and eat.

3. Dress for comfort on your flight; wear loose-fitting clothes.

4. Take advantage of anything that can add to your travel comfort—neck pillows, eyeshades, earplugs, blankets—and remember that an exciting book can help pass the time very quickly. The bigger the print, the easier the book will be on the eyes!

5. Try to avoid heavy meals.

6. Drink lots of water, but skip alcohol and caffeine.

7. Stretch your legs with strolls up and down the aisle. Stretch the rest of your body with isometrics in your seat.

8. Use lubricating drops to combat tired, dry eyes.

9. When you arrive, DON'T plan a major meeting at a time when you would normally be asleep, especially if you need to be alert for a negotiating session.

10. Whenever you can, take daytime flights so you can arrive at your destination at bedtime.

11. Ideally, plan to arrive a day early and rest up before getting down to business.

12. Take along pictures of family and friends, your kid's latest drawing, and your favorite slippers. Though they take up space, these familiar items will help you keep oriented to your "home base."

Part X

The Tool Kit

Tool Kit: A set of materials needed to carry out your occupation.

That is what the 8 charts in Part X are all about *and* you are officially authorized to duplicate them. That way, you'll never be at a loss for those many different forms—the assignment planners, working calendars, ledgers, graph sheets, flow charts, media analyzers and marketing wheels—that you always needed but never had around.

Decisions and Actions

What	Who	When	✔

71

Working Calendar

Action	Sun.	Mon.	Tues.	Wed.	Thurs.	Fri.	Sat.

Planning Ledger

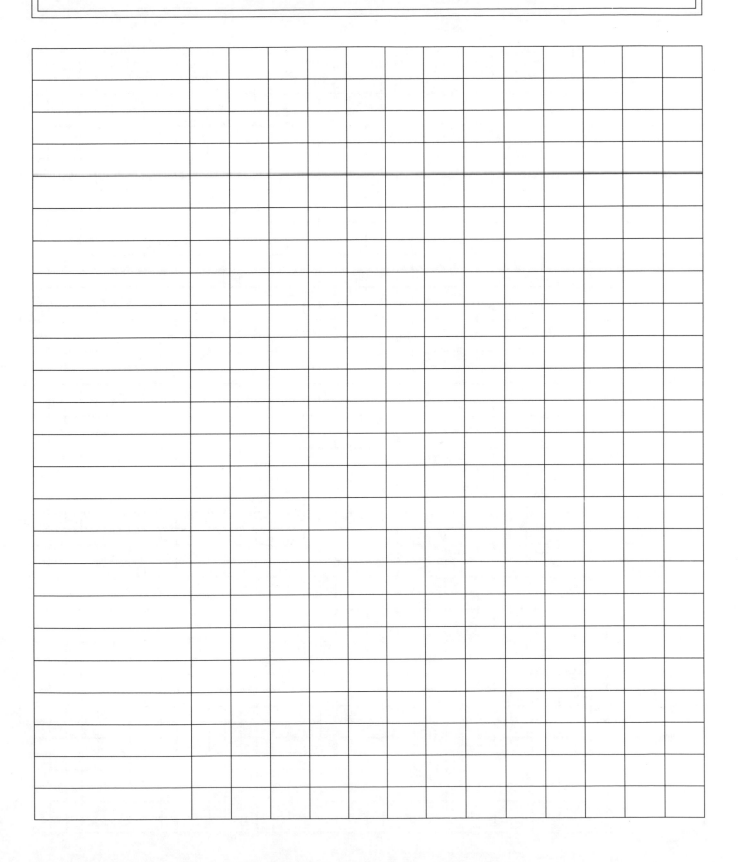

Strategic Plotter

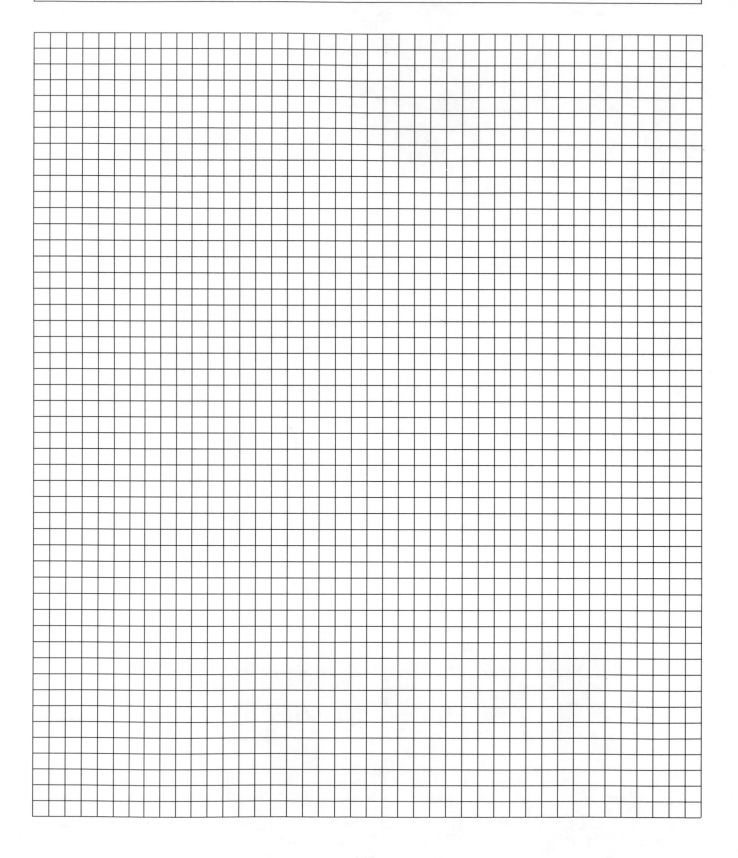

Flow Chart

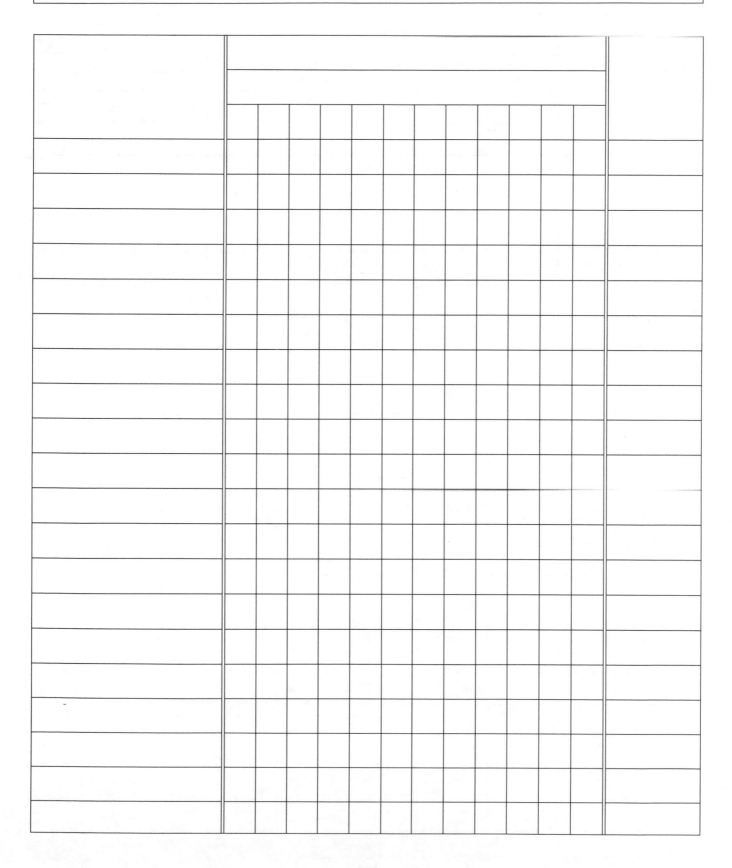

75

Competitive Media Analyzer

Company or Product

Magazines	News-papers	Network TV	Spot TV	Network Radio	Spot Radio	Cable TV	Outdoor	Total

U.S. Market Planner

TELEVISION HOUSEHOLDS						
ADI RANK	**ADI MARKET**	**'000**	**%**			
1	New York	6944.4	7.72			
2	Los Angeles	4807.7	5.34			
3	Chicago	3068.6	3.41			
4	Philadelphia	2642.6	2.94			
5	San Francisco	2164.1	2.40			
6	Boston	2046.1	2.27			
7	Detroit	1712.6	1.90			
8	Dallas-Ft. Worth	1676.7	1.86			
9	Washington, DC	1538.9	1.71			
10	Houston	1447.8	1.61			
		28049.5	31.16			
11	Cleveland	1420.1	1.58			
12	Atlanta	1315.9	1.46			
13	Minneapolis-St. Paul	1307.2	1.45			
14	Miami	1259.9	1.40			
15	Seattle-Tacoma	1255.0	1.39			
16	Pittsburgh	1186.8	1.32			
17	Tampa-St. Petersburg	1181.6	1.31			
18	St. Louis	1104.7	1.23			
19	Denver	1032.2	1.15			
20	Phoenix	959.7	1.07			
		40072.6	44.52			
21	Sacramento-Stockton	957.4	1.06			
22	Baltimore	916.3	1.02			
23	Hartford-New Haven	883.1	0.98			
24	San Diego	836.3	0.93			
25	Orlando-Daytona Beach-Mel	827.5	0.92			
26	Indianapolis	816.8	0.91			
27	Portland, OR	793.1	0.88			
28	Milwaukee	747.9	0.83			
29	Cincinnati	737.4	0.82			
30	Kansas City	731.5	0.81			
		48319.9	53.68			
31	Charlotte	708.5	0.79			
32	Nashville	698.3	0.78			
33	Columbus, OH	667.6	0.74			
34	Raleigh-Durham	660.4	0.73			
35	New Orleans	641.9	0.71			
36	Greenville-Spartanburg-Ash	634.5	0.70			
37	Grand Rapids-Kalam-Battle	609.9	0.68			
38	Buffalo	608.6	0.68			
39	Oklahoma City	607.4	0.67			
40	Salt Lake City	590.4	0.66			
		54747.4	60.82			

Source: Arbitron Ratings Company (1988-1989)

TELEVISION HOUSEHOLDS						
ADI RANK	**ADI MARKET**	**'000**	**%**			
41	Memphis	586.5	0.65			
42	Norfolk-Portsmouth-Newport-Hampt	556.7	0.62			
43	San Antonio	554.1	0.62			
44	Providence-New Bedford	548.4	0.61			
45	Harrisburg-York-Lancaster-Leb	538.0	0.60			
46	Louisville	531.7	0.59			
47	Birmingham	516.2	0.57			
48	Greensboro-Winston-High Poin	509.9	0.57			
49	Dayton	491.7	0.55			
50	West Palm-Ft. Pierce-Vero	490.1	0.54			
		60070.7	66.74			
51	Charleston-Huntington	488.1	0.54			
52	Wilkes Barre-Scranton	485.2	0.54			
53	Albany-Schenectady-Troy	483.3	0.54			
54	Tulsa	460.9	0.51			
55	Little Rock	455.9	0.51			
56	Albuquerque	451.5	0.50			
57	Jacksonville	449.8	0.50			
58	Flint-Saginaw-Bay City	433.2	0.48			
59	Wichita-Hutchinson	432.1	0.48			
60	Knoxville	426.7	0.47			
		64637.4	71.81			
61	Richmond	426.6	0.47			
62	Fresno-Visalia	419.9	0.47			
63	Mobile-Pensacola	410.4	0.46			
64	Toledo	404.6	0.45			
65	Shreveport-Texarkana	403.9	0.45			
66	Des Moines	380.1	0.42			
67	Green Bay-Appleton	375.1	0.42			
68	Syracuse	368.8	0.41			
69	Austin, TX	353.4	0.39			
70	Roanoke-Lynchburg	353.3	0.39			
		68533.5	76.14			
71	Rochester, NY	350.9	0.39			
72	Omaha	349.7	0.39			
73	Portland-Poland Spring	345.1	0.38			
74	Springfield-Decatur-Champ	331.9	0.37			
75	Lexington	328.1	0.36			
76	Paducah-Cp Girardeau-Harr	326.9	0.36			
77	Spokane	323.3	0.36			
78	Cedar Rapid-Waterloo-Dub	313.3	0.35			
79	Davenprt-Rock Islnd-Molin	306.8	0.34			
80	Huntsville-Decatur-Floren	300.5	0.33			
		71810.0	79.77			

TELEVISION HOUSEHOLDS						
ADI RANK	ADI MARKET	'000	%			
81	Tucson	299.8	0.33			
82	Springfield, MO	295.3	0.33			
83	Chattanooga	291.3	0.32			
84	South Bend-Elkhart	289.2	0.32			
85	Jackson, MS	287.9	0.32			
86	Columbia, SC	281.2	0.31			
87	Bristl-Kngspt-Johnsn Cty-	280.8	0.31			
88	Johnstown-Altoona	279.1	0.31			
89	Youngstown	275.6	0.31			
90	Madison	268.7	0.30			
		74658.9	82.93			
91	Evansville	261.6	0.29			
92	Burlington-Plattsburgh	257.6	0.29			
93	Baton Rouge	256.6	0.29			
94	Las Vegas	256.4	0.28			
95	Lincoln-Hastings-Kearney	253.1	0.28			
96	Springfield, MA	242.0	0.27			
97	Waco-Temple	239.1	0.27			
98	Ft. Myers-Naples	235.4	0.26			
99	Colorado Springs-Pueblo	229.2	0.25			
100	Sioux Falls-Mitchell	227.3	0.25			
		77117.2	85.66			
101	Ft. Wayne	225.2	0.25			
102	El Paso	224.5	0.25			
103	Savannah	224.1	0.25			
104	Augusta	222.0	0.25			
105	Lansing	220.6	0.25			
106	Greenville-New Bern-Wash	219.8	0.24			
107	Montgomery-Selma	214.5	0.24			
108	Charleston, SC	212.8	0.24			
109	Fargo	212.7	0.24			
110	Peoria-Bloomington	208.1	0.23			
		79301.5	88.10			
111	Salinas-Monterey	205.6	0.23			
112	Snta Brbra-Snta Maria-Sn	202.0	0.22			
113	Lafayette, LA	198.0	0.22			
114	McAllen-Brownsville-Lrgv	189.2	0.21			
115	Columbus, GA	185.3	0.21			
116	Amarillo	184.8	0.21			
117	Tallahassee-Thomasville	183.0	0.20			
118	Monroe-El Dorado	182.0	0.20			
119	Reno	180.0	0.20			
120	Eugene	179.5	0.20			
		81190.9	90.20			

TELEVISION HOUSEHOLDS						
ADI RANK	ADI MARKET	'000	%			
121	Joplin-Pittsburg	176.6	0.20			
122	Corpus Christi	174.2	0.19			
123	Duluth-Superior	169.8	0.19			
124	Tyler-Longview	169.0	0.19			
125	Terre Haute	167.9	0.19			
126	Beaumont-Port Arthur	165.2	0.18			
127	Yakima	164.4	0.18			
128	Sioux City	164.2	0.18			
129	La Crosse-Eau Claire	163.5	0.18			
130	Macon	163.0	0.18			
		82868.7	92.06			
131	Columbus-Tupelo	162.3	0.18			
132	Florence, SC	161.4	0.18			
133	Wausau-Rhinelander	160.1	0.18			
134	Traverse City-Cadillac	159.4	0.18			
135	Wichita Falls-Lawton	159.3	0.18			
136	Binghamton	157.2	0.17			
137	Boise	155.6	0.17			
138	Topeka	155.4	0.17			
139	Rockford	154.5	0.17			
140	Ft. Smith	153.7	0.17			
		84447.6	93.81			
141	Erie	153.2	0.17			
142	Wheeling-Steubenville	152.7	0.17			
143	Chico-Redding	150.6	0.17			
144	Bluefield-Beckley-Oak Hil	150.2	0.17			
145	Bakersfield	149.9	0.17			
146	Odessa-Midland	148.1	0.16			
147	Rochester-Mason City-Aust	142.6	0.16			
148	Minot-Bismarck-Dickinson	139.8	0.16			
149	Wilmington	139.2	0.15			
150	Lubbock	136.3	0.15			
		85910.2	95.44			
151	Columbia-Jefferson City	131.3	0.15			
152	Medford	130.9	0.15			
153	Albany, GA	129.3	0.14			
154	Quincy-Hannibal	121.6	0.14			
155	Sarasota	118.2	0.13			
156	Abilene-Sweetwater	116.5	0.13			
157	Bangor	114.1	0.13			
158	Biloxi-Gulfport-Pascagoul	110.5	0.12			
159	Dotham	106.0	0.12			
160	Idaho Falls-Pocatello	102.5	0.11			
		87091.1	96.76			

	TELEVISION HOUSEHOLDS					
ADI RANK	ADI MARKET	'000	%			
161	Utica	101.7	0.11			
162	Clarksburg-Weston	94.0	0.10			
163	Salisbury	90.6	0.10			
164	Billings-Hardin	90.6	0.10			
165	Laurel-Hattiesburg	90.2	0.10			
166	Alexandria, LA	87.8	0.10			
167	Gainesville	84.9	0.09			
168	Rapid City	84.3	0.09			
169	Elmira	83.8	0.09			
170	Greenwood-Greenville	80.9	0.09			
		87979.9	97.73			
171	Panama City	79.6	0.09			
172	Watertown-Carthage	78.9	0.09			
173	Lake Charles	75.7	0.08			
174	Missoula	75.5	0.08			
175	Ardmore-Ada	74.4	0.08			
176	Jonesboro	68.5	0.08			
177	Meridian	66.7	0.07			
178	Palm Springs	66.2	0.07			
179	Grand Junction-Durango	64.8	0.07			
180	Jackson, TN	63.0	0.07			
		88693.2	98.51			
181	El Centro-Yuma	62.5	0.07			
182	Great Falls	60.4	0.07			
183	Parkersburg	58.8	0.07			
184	Marquette	55.4	0.06			
185	Tuscaloosa	53.4	0.06			
186	Cheyenne-Scottsbluff-Ster	52.4	0.06			
187	Eureka	51.4	0.06			
188	Butte	48.3	0.05			
189	St. Joseph	47.8	0.05			
190	San Angelo	47.7	0.05			
		89231.3	99.11			
191	Casper-Riverton	45.6	0.05			
192	Anniston	44.7	0.05			
193	Bowling Green	44.1	0.05			
194	Lafayette, IN	42.3	0.05			
195	Roswell	41.7	0.05			
196	Hagerstown	41.2	0.05			
197	Lima	40.6	0.05			
198	Charlottesville	39.3	0.04			
199	Harrisonburg	34.7	0.04			
200	Laredo	34.7	0.04			
		89640.2	99.58			

U.S. Market Planner

TELEVISION HOUSEHOLDS						
ADI RANK	ADI MARKET	'000	%			
201	Zanesville	31.4	0.03			
202	Twin Falls	31.0	0.03			
203	Presque Isle	29.2	0.03			
204	Ottumwa-Kirksville	28.9	0.03			
205	Flagstaff	28.2	0.03			
206	Victoria	25.8	0.03			
207	Bend	25.6	0.03			
208	Mankato	23.0	0.03			
209	Helena	19.0	0.02			
210	North Platte	18.5	0.02			
		89900.8	99.86			
211	Alpena	15.2	0.02			
212	Glendive	6.0	0.01			
		89922.0	99.89			

77

The Multi-Factor
Marketing Wheel

One of the most effective ways to visually demonstrate how various factors are related or impact upon an event is to show them as spokes on a wheel. *The Multi-Factor Marketing Wheel* may be used for this purpose.

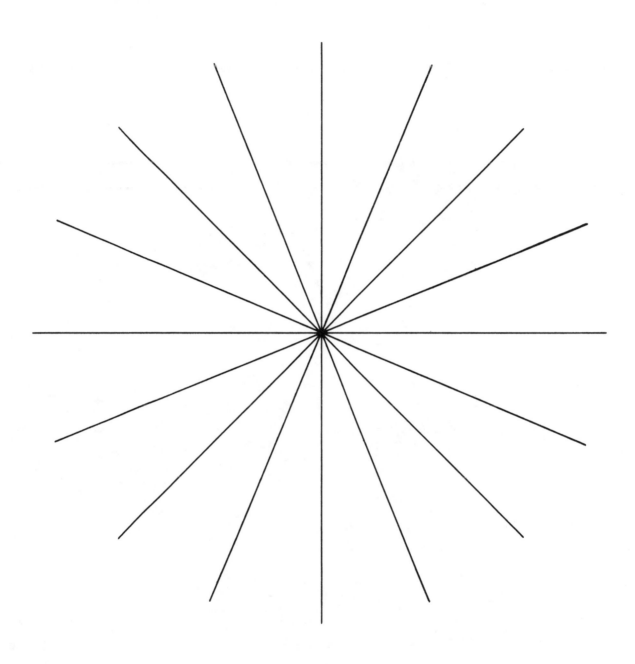

TITLES OF INTEREST IN
PRINT AND BROADCAST MEDIA
FROM NTC BUSINESS BOOKS

Contact: 4255 West Touhy Avenue
            Lincolnwood, IL 60646-1975
            800-323-4900 (in Illinois, 312-679-5500)

Essentials of Media Planning, Second Edition, by Arnold M. Barban, Steven M. Cristol, and Frank J. Kopec

Strategic Media Planning by Kent M. Lancaster and Helen E. Katz

Media Math by Robert W. Hall

Media Planning, Second Edition, by Jim Surmanek

Advertising Media Planning, Third Edition, by Jack Z. Sissors and Lincoln Bumba

How to Produce Effective TV Commercials, Second Edition, by Hooper White

Cable Advertiser's Handbook, Second Edition, by Ron Kaatz

The Radio and Television Commercial, Second Edition, by Albert C. Book, Norman D. Cary, and Stanley Tannenbaum

Children's Television by Cy Schneider

How to Create Effective TV Commercials, Second Edition, by Huntley Baldwin

Fundamentals of Copy and Layout by Albert C. Book and C. Dennis Schick

How to Create and Deliver Winning Advertising Presentations by Sandra Moriarty and Tom Duncan

How to Write a Successful Advertising Plan by James W. Taylor

Advertising Copywriting, Sixth Edition, by Philip Ward Burton

The Art of Writing Advertising by Denis Higgins

Strategic Advertising Campaigns, Third Edition, by Don E. Schultz

Writing for the Media by Sandra Pesmen

The Advertising Portfolio by Ann Marie Barry

Public Relations in the Marketing Mix by Jordan Goldman

Handbook for Business Writing by L. Sue Baugh, Maridell Fryar, and David A. Thomas

Handbook for Public Relations Writing by Thomas Bivins

Handbook for Memo Writing by L. Sue Baugh

How to Write a Successful Marketing Plan by Roman G. Hiebing, Jr., and Scott W. Cooper

NTC Business Books
a division of *NTC Publishing Group*